THE ART of SELF-REGULATION

A Practical Guide to Inner Balance

NICOLETA DRAGAN

DinCali Publishing

Published in 2026 by DinCali Publishing

Paperback ISBN: 979-8-9930722-1-0

eBook ISBN: 979-8-9930722-0-3

First Edition

Cover design by Alex Henning

Cover art direction by fleck creative studio

Interior design and layout by Zara Thatcher

Copy editing by Jessica Brown

Proofreading by Kerry Walters

To those who wrestle with the storms within,
seeking the quiet harmony of balance,
may this book be a gentle guide on your journey.

CONTENTS

INTRODUCTION

"Great books help you understand, and they help you feel understood."

John Green

Going through the adventure of life isn't exactly rainbows and unicorns. In fact, we can be faced with challenges at any point in our life. Regardless of who we are—young, old, poor, rich, good looking, average looking, short, or tall—we are all human beings, and part of the human experience is encountering discomfort, pain, and suffering. If you have ever moved to a new house, neighborhood, or town; experienced the death of a loved one; gone through a separation or divorce; ended a friendship; faced conflict with family, friends, or colleagues; dealt with an unrealistic workload or an insecure job; had to make choices regarding your career path; not had enough money to pay the bills; had to study; taken an exam; failed an exam; got into an accident; received a medical diagnosis; suffered with an illness; lived with a chronic condition; or are a caregiver for someone who needs constant care, you already know that these types of situations can create a tornado of thoughts, emotions, and behaviors that can be very difficult to contain.

Although we all have the desire to go through these challenges with poise and ease, we might fall short in our attempts, ending up feeling defeated and discouraged. If that is your experience, know that you are not alone. We human beings are not born with self-regulation skills—the ability to remain composed when we are upset, stay focused amid distractions, and stick to goals when things get tough. Actually, as children, we need the support of others to help us navigate life's challenges. Without this support, we are left at the mercy of strong physiological and emotional reactions, unable to manage difficult situations. We then become adults who continue to struggle during times of instability, blaming ourselves for our inability to modulate our emotions, thoughts, and behaviors, without realizing this is not a personal flaw but rather a lack of self-regulation capability.

The good news is that self-regulation is a learned skill. It is an ability we can develop with intention at any time in our life. We can learn and practice effective self-regulation strategies to modulate the intensity of our emotions, reshape a harsh internal dialogue into a more caring and supportive one, and positively influence our behavior. Self-regulation is not a magic wand that solves our problems, but it can help us avoid creating unnecessary ones by bringing us moments of ease when faced with life challenges. For that reason, developing our capacity for self-regulation can play a significant role in the quality of our life. Think of self-regulation as a seatbelt that keeps us safe on life's bumpy rides.

My own journey to self-regulation

My anchor in life was never a place or thing, but the people around me: my mother's listening ears, genuinely curious about my experiences; my father's playfulness and constant invitations to explore and push my limits; my sister's wisdom guiding my steps as I was discovering the world; my grandmother's face lighting up whenever she looked at me, always ready to show her love just the way I needed it; my great-grandmother's storytelling about old times while we played cards; my aunts' and uncles' fun presence, warm hugs, and sincere enthusiasm for my accomplishments; my cousins' readiness for new adventures and shenanigans that turned ordinary days into unforgettable memories. Together, they were my safety, my foundation, the ones who made me feel loved and cared about.

I was around eight years old when, out of nowhere, I got really sick. So sick that my parents thought they might lose me. They drove me to the best hospital in the region, a university hospital, which was in a different town and where I was immediately hospitalized for a couple of weeks for an internal infection caused by a parasite. At that time, parents weren't allowed to stay in the hospital with their children, so for the first time in my life, I found myself completely alone, stripped from the safety and comfort of my home environment, with no one to hold and soothe me in the most vulnerable time of my life up to that point.

Back then, the hospitals were not the modern places they are now, and they were even worse in the undeveloped communist Romania where I was living at that time. Transportation, just like many other things in the communist regime, was also an issue, but my parents and extended family members always found ways to visit me on the weekends during visiting hours, the only time they were allowed. I was incredibly fortunate that my mom's cousin was the university librarian; she would sneak in every day to see me and bring me homemade food, which helped tremendously, even if just for a few minutes each day.

In the years that followed, I rarely thought or talked about my experience in the hospital. It wasn't an intentional decision; life just continued to happen, and I was living other experiences. On the rare occasions I would talk about it, it was mostly from the perspective of others—how my body was giving up as my parents were speeding to get me to the hospital, how scary it was for everyone to know that I was in such a critical condition, or how much the medical staff loved me. Every now and then, I would talk about it from my point of view, mostly sharing the same three experiences. The one I talked about the most was the experience of having a tube forced down my throat. Another was my last night there—a sleepless night filled with fun, spent with my two hospital roommates. The third was about the day a teacher came and attempted, unsuccessfully, to do school activities with us.

One day, I casually mentioned to my therapist that I was hospitalized as a child. To my surprise, she didn't join me in my laughter as I reminisced about my fun final night there, spent giggling quietly with my roommates. Instead, with genuine concern and curiosity, she wanted to learn more about my experience. That was the moment I started to process the experience I had never revisited since I was a child. With my adult brain, plenty of resources, and within the emotional safety provided by my therapist, I took my first steps into the memory line of that painful time of my life. I was in a really good place, with enough knowledge and therapeutic support to know that I could face whatever might arise from this process.

In between the therapy sessions, I started journaling about my memories of that time. The intention was to provide myself with the space to hold my experience in mindful awareness without any judgment. With this new created space, fragmented memories started to emerge one by one—the cold rooms; the blue neon tube lights in the hallways, poking into the darkness of the room during the night; the echoes of the nurses' steps on the cement floor; and the crib-like beds with metal bars that were lifted at night, perhaps to keep us children from falling out.

I don't recall much about the daytimes, but I remember the nights. They were the hardest, especially in the beginning, when my body was weak and hooked up to the intravenous line pouring medication directly into my veins. I was alone in an unfamiliar place, surrounded by strangers dressed in white coats who firmly told me that if I kept crying and moving, they would have to tie me to the bed. I didn't want to be tied down, so I did my best to stay still. Another reason I made an effort to stay still was because with each movement I could feel the needle moving in my arm, a sensation that makes me nauseous to this day. There were times when the medical staff would come into the room and poke my arms with thick reusable metal syringes that had been sterilized in boiling water. There were two instances when they held me tight and inserted a tube through my mouth all the way into my stomach to collect a sample of fluid to be sent to the lab. They never asked my permission for any of these invasive procedures. Not that I would have resisted in any way—I was too weak and too scared to protest. I was just a child. There was no resistance, just deep despair, pain, and silent crying, with no one to hold and soothe me. I was completely alone.

Those feelings of deep loneliness and despair haunted me for decades. It was during my journaling sessions that I started noticing a familiar but unwanted physiological reaction to those memories, followed by unpleasant emotions. I observed the tears of silent crying as they would fall over my face, the feelings of weakness in my body, and the deep loneliness and despair making their way into my awareness. The more I was observing and reflecting on those memories, the more aware I became of how much my past was bleeding into my present. A common cold, discomfort or pain in my body, a routine visit to the doctor, or some ordinary blood work was immediately followed by feelings of sadness, loneliness, and even despair, sometimes lasting for weeks. That lived experience of helplessness in the hospital continued to influence my emotions and behavior without my conscious awareness. Twenty years of unwanted fearful reactions and emotional pain making me think that something was wrong with me.

The awareness that sadness and loneliness could sneak up on me at any sign of physical weakness was life changing for me. This newly gained awareness helped me move toward actionable steps that would keep me anchored in the present moment instead of being sucked into the tornado of emotions rooted in the memories of that past experience. To this day, my brain continues to predict the worst-case scenarios based on that early experience. However, I have developed my ability to stay anchored in the present moment and respond to my fears with kindness and support instead of despair and isolation, and to modulate the intensity and duration of those fearful episodes. I still have surges of fear; however, they never last more than a day or two, maybe a few days if I catch the flu or have a more severe injury.

Each new experience of going through episodes of distress without losing myself in them strengthened my trust in myself—that I can find ease in whatever situation I might encounter. I have enough awareness and self-regulation strategies to support me in difficult moments, and knowing I have the ability to regulate my body, my thoughts, and my emotions significantly improved my quality of life.

The reason I wrote this book

This book emerged from my own experience, guided by science. I wrote this book with the intention of sharing the information I have found useful in both my personal and professional life. I am a licensed psychotherapist, and over the years I have witnessed profound transformations that started with the understanding and practice of self-regulation. I discovered it is the quiet power of self-regulation in moments of stress, fear, or conflict that helps us pause before reacting, take a break before speaking, or stay present when wanting to shut down or run away. It is the ability to self-soothe and stay grounded in times of distress that offers us the internal stability we need to effectively navigate life's challenges.

So I wrote this book for those who struggle with self-regulation. Guiding others toward emotional wellbeing has been the focus of my professional life for over a decade, and over time I have learned that when we navigate life's ups and downs with balance, stories of love, kindness, and connection start to emerge. Self-regulation is not a fix for life's problems, but it is an ability that can help us move toward a more intentional future.

I see life itself as a work of art that we have the power to create. The *"ART"* in *The ART of Self-Regulation* symbolizes this idea that we are the creators of our own lives, able to shape and transform our experiences. I built this framework on three main elements essential for a balanced life: **anchoring, reflecting,** and **transforming. Anchoring** refers to the ability to ground in the present moment instead of being caught in the sorrows of the past or worries of the future. **Reflecting** is the process of acknowledging our internal world and examining our experiences with genuine curiosity rather than judgment or criticism. **Transforming** entails taking intentional steps in creating experiences that serve us best. These three elements are designed to guide us in navigating life with intention and ease.

I hope this book will serve as a source of guidance, inspiration, and hope for those who struggle maintaining or regaining internal stability in the face of challenges. I want you to know *you can* build an internal source of balance and comfort you can always rely on. The inability to self-regulate is not a character flaw; it is a lack of knowledge and practice. This book offers both the knowledge and the practical guidance you need to create balance from within.

How to read this book

This book has two parts, both necessary in the process of developing capacity for self-regulation. Part 1 introduces essential information needed to understand the factors that shape us into who we are and why we do what we do, setting the stage for the second part of the book, the experiential part, with practical exercises and tools designed to help integrate your newly acquired knowledge into real-life experiences.

Part 1

The first part of the book is structured into seven chapters, which build upon each other. The information included in each chapter is gathered from scientific research on topics such as attachment, brain functions, shame, and self-compassion. I have also included stories intended to deepen your understanding of the concepts presented in each chapter. All narratives drawn from real-life experiences have been adapted, and any identifying information has been altered to maintain confidentiality.

The aim of part one of the book is to develop your awareness of:

- The foundational factors that shape who we are

- What influences our thoughts, emotions, and behavior

- The factors that contribute to regulation and dysregulation

- Why the inability to self-regulate might feel like a character flaw rather than a lack of knowledge

The knowledge you'll gain in part one builds the foundations you'll need for the guided practice in the second part of the book.

Part 2

The second part of the book introduces the practical elements of the ART of self-regulation—anchoring, reflecting, and transforming—over a 21-day guided experience. The first seven days are tailored to guide you through the process of anchoring in the present moment. Then, for another seven days, you will engage in the process of reflection, designed to examine your experiences and internal world with genuine curiosity and care. Finally, the last seven days have been created to support you in the process of transforming through new experiences.

The experiential activities presented over the 21 days of practice establish the foundation of a lifelong self-regulation adventure that you will keep building on based on your needs. This part of the book includes some written reflection exercises, so you will need a notebook, your favorite pen, and a space with no or minimal distractions.

This is a gift you are offering yourself

You are here, reading this book, choosing to learn and do something meaningful for yourself. This is no small thing. Healing journeys of self-discovery are filled with the unknown, and they can be unsettling at times. This one is no different. There might be times when you face challenges and unpleasant feelings—that's all part of the experience. When that happens, you might find yourself wanting to slow down or seek additional support such as individual or group psychotherapy. There might also be times when you feel seen, heard, and understood, with pleasant feelings unfolding—that's also part of the experience. Acknowledge and savor those positive moments, since they can have a lasting impact on your wellbeing.

There is no right or wrong way of going through this experiential process of developing your self-regulation capacity. This is your journey, and you can do it at your own pace and based on your unique needs. No one knows you better than you know yourself. Only you truly understand your needs, your pain, your desires, and your joys. Only you know what you've been through and why you've made the choices you've made. Only you hold the full story of who you are, with all your complexities and nuances. My hope is that becoming aware of this inspires you to trust your own insights and guide yourself through this process in a way that feels right for you.

When you're ready, buckle up. You're in for a treat!

PART 1

Foundational Knowledge

Chapter 1

Why Embark on a Journey to Self-Regulation?

"Part of emotional intelligence is regulation."

Dr. Marc Brackett

Self-regulation is a foundational skill that supports a sense of balance in all aspects of life. The multidimensional process of self-regulation brings awareness of our body's sensations, the emotional meaning we assign to them, the thoughts that shape our internal dialogue, and the behaviors that follow those thoughts. This awareness helps us make sense of our experiences and informs our actions, helping us choose the most appropriate steps to support a state of internal stability in various situations.

Self-regulation is not an ability we are born with—it is a capacity we build as we develop, and it can continue to grow throughout our lives. We can learn and practice self-regulation skills to manage the intensity of our emotions, thoughts, and behavior. The purpose of this chapter is to introduce the concept of self-regulation and highlight the need for self-regulation in handling the unpredictability of life with equilibrium.

Self-regulation was not my strong suit for the first 25 years of my life, and I genuinely thought it was a flaw of mine—I couldn't correct it, no matter how much I wished I could. I didn't know self-regulation was a skill I could learn and develop. People who stayed calm in challenging situations didn't look like they were *doing* something to be calm; rather, it seemed they were born that way. They remained level-headed when things got tough, without getting too shaken or upset. I loved having those people around me. Now, I understand the reason they felt so good to me was because I was anchoring myself in them—their calmness and balance supported my own calmness and balance. In science, we call this **co-regulation**.

As much as I loved having these people around me, I resented the fact my sense of balance was contingent on others. Especially if the source of my dysregulation was the very person I would anchor in for stability and safety. Those were the most painful times for me in every relationship I have ever had—times of dysregulation with no anchor to keep me from coming adrift in the storm of emotions and thoughts, completely carried away by their currents. So I decided to take the matter of stability and balance into my own hands by building a strong foundation to support myself in challenging times. What I really wanted was to be well, regardless of whether someone was or wasn't there to support me. In science, we call this **self-regulation**.

An essential part of my experience with developing my self-regulation capacity was learning that self-regulation is not an inherent quality but rather something we can develop. Once I understood that, I was committed to the process of developing my ability for self-regulation. My journey through the process wasn't linear or smooth. It was one in which I had to revisit unpleasant past experiences, face fears and personal limitations, reshape my internal dialogue, and take intentional actions to create new experiences. In doing so, I've opened myself up to new knowledge, some found in science and the experiences of others, and some within myself.

Revisiting past experiences from an adult perspective was incredibly transformative. First, it allowed me to see things more clearly and with a maturity I didn't have when they occurred, helping me understand why things happened the way they did and why I responded the way I did at that time. With this added maturity and distance of time, I was also able to recognize patterns in my emotions, thoughts, and behavior that I couldn't see before.

The process of reflecting on past episodes of my life revealed enduring worries and fears that have followed me and shaped my present. I had to face and process them in order to lessen their grip and make space for more pleasant experiences. That's how I've learned the power of being kind and supportive toward myself, especially in turbulent times. That's how I've learned the power of anchoring in the present moment through breathing, movement, and the five senses. That's how I've learned that slowing down is not only something that feels good but is necessary for a life lived with balance. That's how I've come to trust that I can live life by savoring it instead of being overwhelmed and consumed by it.

There are still situations where I seek others for comfort and support, and I will always do that. We need each other's presence in times of high stress, grief, or life crises. Developing the ability to self-regulate is not intended to replace leaning on others in difficult times, since nothing can replace a loved one's listening ear, warm hug, or encouraging words. Developing our self-regulation capacity is knowing we are not at the mercy of strong emotions and reactions but in charge of how we choose to live our life.

What is self-regulation?

Self-regulation is a multidimensional process that helps us maintain or regain a sense of stability when faced with adversity. It involves awareness of the body, thoughts, and emotions, as well as the intentional use of effective strategies that support a state of balance. Self-regulation requires awareness of our body's sensations and the meaning we assign to those sensations, since they drive our emotions, thoughts, and actions. We also need to be aware of the quality of our thoughts, as they also influence our behavior and the way we feel about ourselves and others. Although awareness is necessary for the process of self-regulation, it is not sufficient on its own. We also need to be intentional in implementing self-regulation strategies to support our internal equilibrium.

The body, emotions, thoughts, and behaviors are all interconnected, influencing each other in ways that can either support or disrupt our state of internal harmony. They create a feedback loop, where each one impacts the others, either positively or negatively. Let's explore the role each one plays and how they work together in this process.

The body

We'll start with the body, since our whole existence is contained within and influenced by it. The body requires certain basic elements such as adequate nutrition, water, sleep, and movement to perform at its best, and we need to constantly supply them to support its growth, repair, and maintenance. Without them, our body can't effectively carry out its physiological and cognitive processes, which affects our overall physiological and psychological wellbeing. Sometimes, besides these fundamental components, the body requires additional support for optimal performance. This can be in the form of added sensory ingredients, such as a warm bath, pleasant aromas, dim lights, a quiet space, soft music, or the company of a loved one. Only by listening and responding to our body's signals of distress can we provide the support and comfort it needs in various situations.

Awareness of our internal sensations is important, but it's equally important we are aware of the meaning we attach to these sensations, because they drive our actions. For example, discomfort in our stomach can mean we are hungry, nervous, or sick, which are all very different states that require significantly different actions, such as eating, relaxing, or taking over-the-counter medication. Only by paying attention to our body's sensations and accurately interpreting them can we provide it with the appropriate support. If we misinterpret the sensations, we might end up eating when we are nervous or taking medicine when, actually, we need nutritious food. When we accurately interpret our body's cues, we are not only supporting our physical health but also our emotional wellbeing.

Emotions

Our internal sensations are part of the core ingredients of our emotions, just as flour and water are core ingredients of bread. It is the meaning we assign to these sensations that creates our emotions. Therefore, we need to accurately interpret our bodily sensations to ensure we are not confusing our body's signal of distress with an emotional struggle. A common example of how lack of support for the body can be confused with emotional distress is when we feel constantly fatigued, anxious, or irritable, but the root cause is physical, not emotional. For instance, if we don't get enough sleep, eat properly, or are chronically dehydrated, we might start feeling overwhelmed, stressed, or even depressed. If we are not aware of the root cause of our experience, we might start focusing on managing emotions rather than addressing the physical need for rest and care.

Thoughts

The way we feel also influences our thoughts. For example, unpleasant emotions can cloud our judgment, leading us to jump to conclusions based on how we are feeling in the moment. Have you ever felt so anxious or scared that you started to run through worst-case scenarios in your mind? You might have had thoughts such as *If I speak up, people will judge me or think I'm stupid; Something terrible is going to happen;* or *I'll be alone forever and never find a partner*, even when there was no solid reason to believe that. Sometimes we can feel so hopeless we might think, *Nothing ever goes right for me; I always mess things up; I can never do anything right*, even though that is not true for every situation. We can become so focused on what's bothering us that we end up obsessing over one small problem, spiraling into rumination and ignoring any possible solutions.

The same is true in the case of pleasant emotions. They have the power to steer our thoughts toward hope, empathy, or creativity. Have you ever been in a good mood, feeling like anything is possible? That's because when we feel hopeful or confident, our thoughts are more likely to focus on solutions and lead us to think more positively, such as *There is always a way forward and I will find it* or *I can handle this*. I am sure you've noticed that when you feel thankful or content, you tend to shift your thinking toward the pleasant aspects of your life, like having good health, supportive relationships, or the things that bring you joy. Pleasant emotions allow us to be open to new ideas, and thoughts such as *I'm excited to try this and see where it takes me!* or *Every journey begins with a single step and I'm ready to take mine* might emerge. Also, in moments when we feel calm and content, we find it easier to make thoughtful decisions, think through problems, and remain grounded, knowing we can always take one step at a time.

An ongoing stream of thoughts is part of the human experience, and it creates a continuous inner dialogue. This dialogue can be kind, caring, and supportive, and therefore an internal source of ease and comfort, or it can be critical, diminishing, and hurtful, adding suffering to our experience. The conversations we have with ourselves, whether we are aware of them or not, play a significant role in how we behave, as they directly influence how we perceive ourselves, our abilities, and the world around us. Thoughts such as *I can do things differently, Mistakes are part of the learning process,* and *I am worthy of love even when I make mistakes* cultivate a willingness to make adjustments and take risks rather than giving up when things get tough. An encouraging inner reflection also fuels hope that we can manage challenging situations, inspires motivation, and can add a sense of ease in the midst of difficulties.

In contrast, a harsh internal dialogue can lead to self-doubt, procrastination, and reluctance to take risks. When faced with personal limitations, we might notice thoughts such as *I am not good enough, I am too old to change,* and *I can't do this.* These types of thoughts impact our behavior by eroding our confidence and creating a sense of helplessness, which often leads to avoidance and reluctance to pursue opportunities. These critical and discouraging thoughts can also be a source of internal turmoil that adds unnecessary suffering to the difficult situation we are already in. Ultimately, the conversations we have with ourselves guide our decisions, reactions, and interactions with others. For this reason, we need to be mindful of the quality of our self-talk and intentionally shift it toward a more encouraging tone that supports our state of harmony and balance.

The *self* in self-regulation highlights the fundamental idea that we have the power and responsibility to manage and shape our internal experiences. While we are continuously influenced by external factors, we are not passive recipients of those influences. As it turns out, we have the ability to choose how we respond to them. Self-regulation allows us to pause before reacting, taking thoughtful actions rather than impulsive ones. It also helps us recognize when we need rest, when our emotions are overwhelming, or when our thoughts are spiraling out of control. In other words, it provides us with a sense of control over our internal state, actively shaping our day-to-day experiences.

Why do we need self-regulation?

The ability to self-regulate adds a feeling of safety and stability during hard times. Whether it's managing frustration in a heated conversation or staying focused on a long-term goal despite setbacks, self-regulation helps us stay grounded and move through life's challenges with flexibility. When we cultivate self-regulation, we develop the inner strength we need to remain composed under pressure and make thoughtful decisions.

When we develop our self-regulation capacity, we are basically learning to rely on ourselves to handle whatever life throws our way. Imagine being in a heated argument with a friend, and instead of saying things that could damage the relationship and regretting it later, you choose to anchor yourself in your breathing to modulate the intensity of your emotions and reaction. In that moment, you are not relying on the person in front of you to put a stop to the argument but rather on your own self. Each time you successfully navigate such a situation with equilibrium, you strengthen the trust in your ability to manage your emotions and reactions.

Another example could be managing unexpected bad news. Instead of immediately panicking and reacting with fear and worry, you can pause and figure out how to support yourself in that very moment. By doing this, you provide yourself with the opportunity to create space between you and the situation, a space in which you can then think of ways to best approach the situation without becoming consumed by it. You start trusting that you can handle pressure and find solutions without getting overwhelmed.

Self-regulation is not just about maintaining a sense of stability and balance within ourselves in tough moments; it is also about *trusting that we can do it when needed*. Over time, with each successful experience of self-regulation, we start feeling more confident in our ability to handle challenges. It is like training a muscle—we might not see immediate results, but with practice we eventually become more composed and better equipped to deal with life's curveballs in ways that feel good to us and those around us. The more we trust ourselves, the less we need to rely on external support because we can do it on our own.

Although relying on others in difficult moments is appropriate and necessary at times, as adults, we have the responsibility of caring for ourselves. Constantly leaning on friends and family to assist us in regaining balance places an unfair pressure on them, leading to frustration, resentment, or burnout. It also creates a dependence that hinders our own personal growth and emotional maturity, eroding our confidence in ourselves to effectively handle challenges without becoming overwhelmed by them. Of course, it is okay to lean on friends or family for comfort when things get rough, but when we build self-regulation skills, we don't need to put the pressure of our wellbeing on them anymore. Instead, we can rely on ourselves to handle life's twists and turns, ultimately feeling more capable of managing whatever situation we might encounter.

CHAPTER 2

Where It All Begins: Attachment

"We have the kind of nature that requires nurture."

Dr. Lisa Feldman Barrett

For better or worse, our childhood experiences influence our present. Over 80 years of scientific research shows that the way we relate to our own self and the world around us is shaped by our early years. The quality of the relationship we had with our primary caregiver, usually our mother, plays a significant role in how we view the world as adults. This relationship sets the foundation for our emotional and social development, influencing how we navigate the world in adulthood. It is this relationship that shapes our trust in ourselves and others, our sense of worth, and ability to self-regulate.

In this chapter, I will introduce you to the science of attachment, which speaks of the bond between the child and their primary caregiver. When this bond is based on trust, care, and support, it creates a sense of security and connection which, in the science of attachment, is called **secure attachment**. In contrast, when unhealthy dynamics are at play, the result is an **insecure attachment**, which leads to a range of emotional and relational challenges that are carried into adulthood. There are three types of insecure attachment in adulthood: **preoccupied, dismissive**, and **fearful-avoidant**, all telling the story of how we became the person we are.

No matter what our past looks like, we all have certain patterns of vulnerability following us in different ways. Understanding the four attachment styles—secure, preoccupied, dismissive, and fearful-avoidant—can provide great insight into whether our early childhood experiences support us into living a balanced life or if, instead, they lead us into perpetuating unhealthy relational patterns that are hurting us. Awareness of our patterns allows us to understand how the past shapes our present and gives us the opportunity to change how we respond to ourselves and others. Once we can pinpoint how those past experiences are showing up in our lives, we can start to break those cycles and approach relationships and emotional situations from a healthier, more conscious place.

Being a psychotherapist comes with the privilege of being with people at their most vulnerable state, sometimes during the most challenging times of their life. I call it a privilege because I get to witness parts that we tend to hide from each other under masks of charm, shyness, or indifference. Real-life stories of sorrow, heartache, fear, grief, agony, distress, shame, or discomfort buried deeply so no one can see, sometimes not even the person who carries the pain. Hurts endured in isolation and often confused with weakness.

Over the years, I have learned that people who struggle the most have one thing in common: parents who were mostly inconsistent, distant, or unpredictable—that is, who didn't respond to their child's emotional or physical needs, creating a sense of insecurity within their relationship. I will use a simple story to illustrate how the parents' responses to their child's emotional needs can create a sense of security or insecurity within the parent–child relationship, which is then carried into the child's subsequent relationships as they mature and become an adult. This story illustrates the concept of attachment, the bond between the parent and the child, which can be secure or insecure.

Once upon a time, there was a little boy named Ben. Ben had a favorite teddy bear, Mr. Cuddles, which he carried with him everywhere. Mr. Cuddles wasn't just a toy; he was Ben's friend and comfort whenever he felt scared or sad. One day, Ben's mom had to run an errand, and as they walked to the car, Ben realized Mr. Cuddles was missing. His heart sank. He looked everywhere around the house but Mr. Cuddles was nowhere to be found. Ben became upset and called out for his mom. She gently picked him up and reassured him that they would look for Mr. Cuddles together. Although he was a bit nervous, Ben felt comforted the moment his mom held his hand and spoke kindly to him. He wasn't alone. It was the presence of his mom, and her calm reassurance, that helped him feel safe. After a short search, they found Mr. Cuddles under the couch. Ben was very happy, and he hugged his mom and his teddy bear tightly. But more importantly, Ben was reassured that whenever he felt afraid or uncertain, he could always turn to the people who cared for him, like his mom.

Now let's hear a different version of the same story. Once upon a time, there was a little boy named Ben. Ben had a favorite teddy bear, Mr. Cuddles, which he carried with him everywhere. Mr. Cuddles wasn't just a toy; he was Ben's friend and comfort whenever he felt scared or sad. One day, Ben's mom had to run an errand, and as they walked to the car, Ben realized Mr. Cuddles was missing. His heart sank. He looked everywhere around the house, but Mr. Cuddles was nowhere to be found. Ben's mom noticed how upset he was about losing Mr. Cuddles, and she reacted with frustration and impatience: "Ben, you've lost your bear again? How could you be so careless? You need to pay more attention next time!" Ben was already feeling upset, but now he started to feel even more anxious. He started searching for Mr. Cuddles, and the tension in the air made him feel like it was his fault. As he continued looking for Mr. Cuddles, his mom joined him but remained distant, checking the time and sighing, which made Ben feel even more alone and uncertain. "I told you to be more careful, Ben. We don't have time for this," said his mother. When they eventually found the teddy bear, her focus was still on Ben's mistake rather than his emotions: "Well, at least you found it, but you need to stop losing things like that. You can't keep depending on me for everything." In this version of the story, Ben is learning that his emotions are not important, and his distress is burdensome. Instead of feeling reassured and comforted by his mother, he receives the message that he cannot consistently rely on others for comfort when he needs them most. Over time, this could lead to anxiety about whether his needs will be met, causing him to struggle with trusting others to provide him with comfort and security in difficult times.

Over the years, I've heard many versions of Ben's story from adults who struggled in various ways. For example, those preoccupied with and continuously trying to please others at their own expense have shared stories of parents who sometimes responded to their needs in a nurturing way and other times were distant, based on the parent's mood or stress level. So they became hyper-vigilant about others' availability and affection, fearing their needs won't always be met. I witnessed them becoming dysregulated at any sign of conflict in their relationships, ruminating over the fear of being rejected and struggling to maintain or regain inner balance.

I also heard stories of those who described their parents as being indifferent or even irritated when they expressed signs of distress or emotional struggles, leading them to hide their emotions and believe that emotions aren't important. They didn't feel understood by their parents and couldn't seek comfort or help from them in times of vulnerability, because they were pushed toward self-sufficiency and encouraged to handle problems on their own without guidance and support. As a result, they learned to suppress their emotions and become self-reliant, hiding their distress and struggling to share that part of themselves in their relationships.

I've also heard stories of those who experience consuming and complex inner turmoil caused by their parents' unpredictable, abusive, or erratic behavior. These adults have a deep longing for love and safety while, at the same time, feeling haunted by the fear they could be hurt in profound and unpredictable ways by the very person they love and care about. These contradictory feelings come with a deep sense of instability caused by the back-and-forth of wanting closeness but fearing the emotional cost of getting it.

What all these stories have in common is a lack of security that people feel within themselves and in their relationships with others. The same patterns of inconsistency, insecurity, or confusion experienced in their relationship with their parents are now present in their current relationships. Oftentimes, they blame themselves for these unhealthy patterns, not realizing that our childhood experiences "program" us to feel, think, and behave in certain ways.

What is attachment?

Attachment is the bond that develops through the psychological, biological, and behavioral attunement between a child and their primary caregiver. We are biologically wired to seek safety and care from our primary caregivers for survival. Starting in infancy, we need our caregivers to be consistently responsive to our physical and emotional needs. Based on the quality of our caregivers' responsiveness to our needs and signals of distress, our attachment can become secure or insecure. For example, if the primary caregiver responds with sensitivity and warmth toward our needs in infancy, we develop a secure attachment. In contrast, if the primary caregiver is not in sync with our needs, and therefore not a reliable source of comfort, calming, or safety, we develop an insecure attachment.

The four attachment styles

The attachment we develop in infancy can be **secure**, **anxious**, **avoidant**, or **disorganized**. These four attachment styles developed in infancy also have parallels in adulthood; they carry forward into the following corresponding attachment styles: **secure**, **preoccupied**, **dismissive**, and **fearful-avoidant**. Next is a description of all four attachment styles and their influence in adult life.

Secure attachment

A **secure attachment** develops in the context of a consistently safe, caring, and responsive relationship with the primary caregiver. When our caregivers are sensitively attuned and responsive to our needs, we develop a sense of security. For example, you're likely to have a secure attachment if your mother responded to your signs of distress appropriately and in a timely manner, picking you up and using a soothing voice when you were in distress, or encouraged your independent exploration while providing you with support when you needed it.

Having a secure attachment has significant real-life positive implications. For instance, it contributes to feelings of self-worth. Why? Because securely attached people internalize their early experience of consistent love, care, and support from their caregivers, so they believe they are worthy despite their imperfections. For that reason, they are able to recognize and accept both their strengths and weaknesses, without fearing they will be rejected for their limitations. Their early experience of security helped them develop a realistic but positive sense of self and, more importantly, a view of self that remains consistent even in times of distress.

The safety and support provided by their parents also helps them feel more emotionally balanced and have a positive view on life, which translates into better mental health. Because they feel more emotionally steady, they navigate hard times with more ease when things get tough. As a result, they deal with less anxiety and depression than those with insecure attachment. They are also more likely to form stable relationships, which provides them with emotional support, reducing feelings of loneliness and isolation. One reason for their success in relationships is they offer their partner safety through being consistent. They also know how to navigate the nuances of social situations and are very likely to follow social norms. Indeed, they rarely break rules. They are also willing to take other people's ideas into consideration, work collaboratively with others, and when encountering problems in relationships, they handle them with flexibility and persistence while showing empathy for others' struggles.

In essence, secure attachment provides a solid foundation that helps people feel worthy and have close relationships and a positive outlook on life.

Preoccupied attachment

The **preoccupied attachment** style has its roots in the anxious attachment style developed in infancy, which develops when the caregiver is insensitive and inconsistent in their responsiveness toward the infant's distress. For example, caregivers of these children will sometimes respond to and sometimes ignore their children's needs and signals for closeness. When the child is upset, the caregiver will sometimes respond with warmth and hold the child close to their body, while other times they might seem irritated or frustrated by the child's distress.

As these children grow up, the parents continue to respond inconsistently to their needs and often fail to support their independent exploration. This happens because these parents struggle with tolerating their child's distress, often leading them to have intrusive behaviors toward the child. For example, the parent might solve the child's problem rather than allowing them to figure out a way to do it on their own. In real life, that might look like the child getting frustrated trying to tie their shoelaces—instead of encouraging them or offering guidance, the parent quickly steps in and does it for them, not allowing the child to struggle, learn, or feel a sense of accomplishment. Another example could be the parent speaking for the child, immediately answering for them or finishing their sentences in a conversation with another adult, not giving the child space to express themself or build confidence in social situations. After a disappointing experience, like losing a game or not being invited to a party, the parent might try to distract the child from unpleasant emotions by dismissing them with comments like "It's not a big deal," or "You're fine," instead of helping the child work through their feelings.

These children then become preoccupied adults who tend to be overly dependent on others while struggling with low or unstable self-worth. Their sense of value is heavily tied to how others perceive and respond to them, especially in close relationships. Why? Because their early caregiving experiences were filled with inconsistency, so they haven't had a consistent sense of being loved and supported, leading to a persistent need for reassurance and approval from others. As a result, their self-worth can fluctuate dramatically, feeling good about themselves when they feel secure in a relationship but quickly doubting their worth when they sense distance or disapproval. This reliance on external validation makes it difficult for them to develop a stable sense of self-worth.

The constant need for reassurance, and the emotional ups and downs that come with that, can take a toll on their mental health. That can look like calling or sending a text to someone and becoming overwhelmed with worry if they don't answer or reply straight away, immediately wondering if they did something wrong or if the person is upset with them. This kind of constant emotional vigilance can lead to anxiety, low mood, and even burnout over time.

Someone with anxious attachment usually struggles with appropriately regulating their mental and emotional states, often exaggerating their distress or inadequacies in an effort to receive the support, affection, and compassion of others. They don't trust that others can love them, and often ruminate on things, especially during conflict, while holding negative beliefs of both themselves and others. Consequently, their relationships are filled with insecurities and hyper-vigilance, which eventually has an eroding effect.

In essence, preoccupied attachment creates an unstable foundation where self-worth depends heavily on others, relationships feel uncertain, and emotional wellbeing is often tied to fear of rejection and the need for constant reassurance.

Dismissive attachment

The **dismissive attachment** style stems from avoidant attachment developed in infancy. This type of attachment emerges when the parent responds to the infant's distress with anger, intolerance, or active rejection. The parent is usually disengaged from the child, both physically and emotionally, and tends to punish the distressed child instead of providing comfort. This happens because the parent perceives the child as being bad or acting out with the sole intention of irritating them. These parents often express anger or make negative comments about their children and might avoid physical contact.

As these children get older, their parents continue to be emotionally unavailable, critical, or distant. Rather than offering comfort or validating the child's emotions, these parents typically encourage independence to the extreme, discourage emotional expression, and respond to vulnerability with discomfort or disapproval. This ongoing lack of emotional connection teaches the child to suppress their needs and emotions in order to avoid rejection or disappointment. Over time, the child learns to believe that depending on others is unsafe or unproductive, shaping a pattern of emotional detachment that persists into adulthood.

These children then become dismissive adults, meaning they typically suppress their feelings and avoid seeking support. Why? Because they have internalized their caregiver's active rejection and developed an expectation that others are not a source of comfort in difficult times. Their early experiences, in which their attempts to express emotion were met with rejection, discomfort, or indifference, led them to believe that showing vulnerability is a sign of weakness, and relying on others is both risky and pointless. As a result, they keep others at a distance and prioritize independence to protect themselves.

While they might appear confident, their self-worth is fragile because it is built on emotional avoidance rather than a coherent sense of identity. Dismissive adults do not hold a genuine representation of self, tending to inflate their abilities while experiencing self-criticism. To others, this can look like confidence, but beneath the surface their self-worth is often conditional—tied to showing no vulnerability and being in control. As a result, any situation that challenges their independence, like needing help or getting close to someone, can trigger feelings of insecurity, inadequacy, and even shame.

Because they grew up with caregivers who were emotionally distant and critical, they never learned to value emotions. This means that when they avoid or disconnect from their or others' emotional needs, it is not necessarily because they don't care; they simply might not see value in them. Eventually, this avoidance of and disconnection from emotions can lead to unexplained feelings of emptiness. Although they might appear to be self-contained and unbothered, they do experience distress.

In stressful times, dismissive people protect themselves by keeping emotional distance and acting self-reliant. In such situations, they hide their vulnerability by exaggerating their positive characteristics and minimizing their limitations out of fear that if their inadequacies are discovered, they will be rejected. Because they expect to be rejected, they withdraw from others before that can happen, ironically creating the very loneliness and disconnection they were trying to avoid. In the long run, this attitude negatively impacts their relationships because their behavior is often misinterpreted as arrogant and self-sufficient.

While they may genuinely care about others, their protective emotional walls can make it hard for people to feel truly connected to them. For instance, in romantic relationships, a dismissive partner might avoid serious conversations or shut down their significant other's attempts to express emotional needs by saying things like "You're too sensitive" or "I don't see why we need to talk about this again." In friendships, they might be friendly and engaging on the surface but rarely open up about their own struggles, preferring to keep things surface level. Even in moments when they truly need closeness, like during a challenging life situation, they might withdraw or act like everything is fine, because they learned early in life that relying on others is not welcomed or safe.

In essence, dismissive attachment creates an apparent stable foundation—a superficial sense of confidence built on emotional distance, where self-worth is maintained through independence, while intimacy and vulnerability are avoided for self-protection.

Fearful-avoidant attachment

Finally, the **fearful-avoidant attachment** style is the result of a disorganized attachment developed in infancy. This type of attachment develops within a confusing child–parent relationship where the parent is a source of both comfort and terror. These parents often have extreme contradictory behaviors and become abusive and neglectful, which is frightening to the child. These behaviors could be rooted in the parent's own unresolved attachment trauma, such as the loss of a parent, abuse, or neglect, but also from substance abuse or mental illness like severe depression or bipolar disorder.

Unfortunately, due to their own unresolved problems, these parents are at high risk of neglecting and maltreating their children. So, for these children, the need for closeness to their caregivers creates a profound internal conflict—while they crave the comfort and security of their caregiver, they are simultaneously terrified by their very presence and, as a consequence, the children end up experiencing fright without resolution. Simply put, these children are in a continuous state of dysregulation. Their distress might look like odd and out-of-context behavior, as well as distressed emotional expression, such as confusion, fear, or appearing to be in a trance. They might seem disoriented, moving very slowly or remaining completely still, or have rapid and almost simultaneous conflicting behaviors such as laughing and crying at the same time.

These children become fearful-avoidant adults, meaning they can feel overwhelmed by closeness or intimacy, yet isolated without it, often sending mixed signals of wanting closeness while pulling away at the same time. Why? Because they learned early on from their caregivers that love is tied to fear, that people who are supposed to protect you will also hurt you. So when they get too close to others and become vulnerable, they protect themselves by withdrawing, acting cold, or putting up walls, even when they don't actually want to.

Although fearful-avoidant people crave love and connection, they are too scared of getting hurt and end up in a push-and-pull loop where they are pulling people in just to push them away when they get close. For example, they might drop their emotional guard one day and go silent the next, not because they don't care but because being close brings up the fear of being deeply hurt or even abandoned. Such a push–pull dynamic can be intense, unstable, and emotionally exhausting, not only for them but also for people close to them. This instability in relationships leaves them feeling lonely and isolated, with a sense that something is deeply wrong with them.

The constant loop of uncertainty, and the emotional highs and lows that come with it, can also make them feel confused, unsure of what is real and what is just their fear. This lack of trust in themselves and others affects all their relationships. For example, after expressing a need or setting a boundary, they might start thinking, *Was I too much? Did I just push them away?* Or if someone doesn't call or text back immediately, they might start wondering, *Did I say something wrong? Am I being needy? Should I back off? Will they leave me now?* When everything is going well or they are starting to feel connected, they might think, *This feels too good to be true. Can I trust this, or am I missing something?* They might even end up retreating from the relationship because, deep down, they are questioning whether they are worthy of the love and care they so deeply desire.

This type of self-doubt happens in friendships as well. For instance, after sharing something vulnerable, they might start wondering whether they shared too much, or if they came across as weird. If they call or text a friend who doesn't respond immediately, they might start questioning, *Am I imagining things, or are they pulling away?*, constantly replaying conversations and wondering whether they did or said something wrong.

In essence, fearful-avoidant attachment is defined by a painful polarity: a confusing mix of craving connection while fearing it, where self-worth is fragile, trust is difficult, and both intimacy and independence feel unsafe.

Insecure attachment does not mean "bad" or "wrong"

Secure and insecure attachments do not mean "good" and "bad" attachments. Rather, they provide us with an understanding of how our early experiences shaped us into who we are today. You might perceive insecure attachment as being something "bad," but it really doesn't mean something is "wrong" with the person that is insecurely attached. It is just the brain's way of wiring to the world. More specifically, it reveals the way one's brain has learned to adapt to their early childhood environment in order to survive. It unintentionally unveils the hardships they faced very early in life. But, more importantly, it reveals the person's ability to adapt to those early life situations and survive the difficulties.

Instead of judging attachment styles as being "good" or "bad," "right" or "wrong," I invite you to look at them as a ticket for the lottery of life. Some lottery tickets might be expensive, and you don't win anything; other tickets might lead to a small win, just enough to cover their cost, while some could result in big wins, including the jackpot. In this analogy, having a secure attachment is like getting a winning ticket in the lottery of life, meaning that, most likely, your early childhood environment supported you to develop internal resources to help you navigate life's challenges. Among others, those resources could be mental and physical health, capacity for self-regulation, and the ability to form close relationships.

In contrast, when you have an insecure attachment, your life lottery ticket has been pretty expensive and with minimal wins or no gain at all attached to it in the first years of your life—meaning your early childhood environment wasn't supportive in developing your internal and external resources to help you effectively navigate life's challenges. In fact, the caregiving environment and the relationships you grew up in were challenging, intrusive, neglectful, unsafe, or abusive. An environment like this would have a negative effect on anyone's mental and physical health, capacity for regulation, and ability to form relationships. This is why you might perceive insecure attachment as being something "bad," but it is simply not. It is just the nervous system's way of adapting to the world.

If, through the information presented in this book, you learn you might have an insecure attachment, please resist the urge to dismiss it or fight it, as might be your instinct. Instead, I invite you to allow this new information to be just as it is, without resisting or judging it. Acknowledging your attachment style might be one of the most important first steps in reassessing your inner and outer resources in a more accurate way, which usually leads to increased security within yourself and in your relationships.

CHAPTER 3

The Predictive Brain

"The brain is a prediction-making machine."

Dr. Andrew Huberman

The brain's main role is to keep us alive and well. At all times and without our conscious awareness, our brain is coordinating regulation processes within our body to ensure our survival. Think of your brain as the commander in chief who controls and coordinates all your body's activities. At any given time, your brain receives information from inside and outside the body, processes the information, and makes executive decisions intended to adapt to the ever-changing conditions. It integrates information from all parts of your body, orchestrates complex behaviors, and shapes how you understand and interact with the world. To do that, it relies on past experiences, present context, and the internal resources available.

To describe the complex processes that take place in the body under the brain's guidance, in this chapter I'm going to introduce you to the **body budget** metaphor. I'm also going to describe the brain's essential role in your wellbeing, how it constructs your reality, and why it is important to accurately identify your emotions. This information is foundational in understanding the basic mechanisms that shape our reality. At the same time, this knowledge is empowering because it allows us to support our physical and psychological wellbeing.

A few years ago, I spent the summer in my home country, Romania. One of my favorite things to do when I am there is to hang out in nature with my family and friends. During this particular summer, I'd heard numerous people saying they had been, or knew someone who had been, bitten by a tick—a parasite found in grassy areas and woodlands that feeds on the blood of humans and animals. The danger that comes with these tick bites is that they can cause Lyme disease, a serious illness that can lead to paralysis and, eventually, death. These stories about tick bites made me hyper-cautious and alert—I was determined to end the summer without a tick bite and not catch Lyme disease.

One day, fully covered in tick-repellent spray, I was enjoying the company of my family and friends in one of the peaceful meadows of the forest that surrounds my hometown. After a midday nap under an old oak tree, I woke up and noticed a tick-like mark on my left hand. I looked at it and my eyes immediately filled with tears. "I got bit by a tick. I got bit by a tick. I can't believe I got bit by a tick," I said with a shaky voice, looking in disbelief at my hand that carried the parasite. Tears were running down my face like a river. Everyone gathered around me; some attempted to comfort me, while others started brainstorming solutions to my situation. One suggestion was to take the tick out of my hand in the traditional way, using a matchstick—a strategy passed down from generation to generation in our community. Another was to rush me to the hospital and let the doctors take care of the situation. During this whole time, I was trying to stay as still as possible, protecting the mark with my right hand, hoping that by doing that, the tick would not get deeper under my skin. I was so terrified by the tiny mark on my hand that I didn't want anyone to get too close and scare the tick deeper under my skin. Finally, my mom took control of the situation, got a matchstick, and asked me to allow her to rub the coated part of the match around the tick to get it out from under my skin. Apparently, ticks don't like the chemicals matchstick tips are coated with, making them an effective tool to extract ticks from under the skin. Luckily for me, we had matches with us! And if you are wondering why someone would have matches in the middle of the Romanian countryside, it is because we would often light a campfire to cook on. Everyone agreed to the plan; therefore, I agreed to it too. To be honest, I would have agreed to anything that would've taken that terrifying little being away from my hand. Before the procedure, with great care, my mom rubbed the skin around the mark with an alcohol-soaked tissue. Apparently, ticks don't like alcohol either. In the process, the tick got stuck on the tissue and as my mom looked closer, she realized the tick was, actually, just a tiny piece of leaf that had got stuck to my hand. I couldn't believe my eyes and ears. At this point, I was feeling relieved and confused at the same time.

This is what happened that day: my very real reality was just a construction of my brain. I was in nature, aware of the stories about the increase in tick bites that year, so when I woke up from my nap and saw the little mark on my hand, my brain automatically translated that into a tick bite. As a consequence, my brain immediately started coordinating changes in my body, such as my heart rate, blood pressure, muscle tension, and other physical responses to support the action I needed to take in that situation of perceived threat. Without my conscious awareness, my brain retrieved information from my memory that was resembling the context I was in, simulated a reality, and prepared my body to react to that simulated reality. How the brain can do that and how it constructs our reality is what you will learn in the next part of this chapter.

The brain's main role is to keep us alive and well

Our brain's most important job is not thinking, feeling, or sensing, as you might think, but rather regulating our very complicated body to ensure its survival. But how does our brain coordinate this great balancing act across all the systems in our body? This is how it unfolds... Our brain lives in a dark place called the skull, so it relies on our body's many sensory systems to provide information about the continuous changes that are happening inside and outside our body. It keeps track of how much energy our cells are using; the levels of glucose, salt, oxygen, and carbon dioxide in our system; and changes in muscle tension, hormone levels, and body temperature. It also monitors all the information coming from the environment through our eyes, ears, nose, mouth, and skin. This continuous stream of information is used by our brain to anticipate our body's needs and the metabolic resources that must be allocated to the various systems of our body to keep us alive.

As you are reading these words, your brain is coordinating your entire body without your conscious awareness of it. Right at this moment, your brain is regulating the energy of billions of cells in your body, supervising about 600 muscles, maintaining the equilibrium of various hormones traveling through your blood, and managing various other interconnected systems such as the immune, digestive, endocrine, and cardiovascular systems. In science, this dynamic process of coordination and regulation of the body by the brain is called **allostasis**.

The body budget

Dr. Lisa Feldman Barrett, a neuroscientist and psychologist, uses the metaphor of a **body budget** to describe allostasis in language accessible to all. In this analogy, the body budget represents the body's metabolic economy of everyday life. More specifically, it describes how the brain is running a metabolic budget for our body by strategically allocating resources within our body to keep us alive. At all times, and beyond our perception, the brain is budgeting and allocating resources, such as water, salt, oxygen, and glucose, as we lose and gain them.

Just like a financial budget, we can make deposits to or withdraw from our body budget. Think of deposits as anything that replenishes the body's resources, such as eating nutritious food, getting enough sleep, exercising, drinking water, relaxing, or being around people you trust and love. Think of withdrawals as everything that spends the body's resources, such as your heartbeat, getting up from bed in the morning, fighting an illness, learning something new, isolation, social stress, any type of change, or situations filled with the unknown.

Some things may be more metabolically expensive than others and can significantly drain our body budget, affecting our wellbeing. If you have ever experienced the uncertainty of a medical diagnosis, the looming threat of losing a job, or the emotional weight of a breakup, you'll know the feeling of being physically drained and mentally overwhelmed. The reason we feel such overwhelm in these situations is because the body and mind work relentlessly to navigate the uncertainty that comes with not knowing what lies ahead. This relentless mental effort is not only highly costly for the body, as it consumes significant internal resources, but it also impairs our ability to replenish those resources, creating a cycle of depletion. For example, the anxiety of a situation may disrupt sleep, diminish our appetite, and ultimately drain our overall energy levels, taking a toll on both our physical and mental wellbeing. The longer the uncertainty, the bigger the cost.

When we provide our body with adequate metabolic resources—meaning we eat an appropriate amount of nutritious food, get consistent and sufficient sleep, exercise, and maintain close relationships—we support both our physical and psychological wellbeing. In contrast, when our body is depleted of metabolic resources due to lack of sleep, loss of a job or a friend, inadequate nutrition, or a sedentary lifestyle, we experience significant physical and psychological discomfort. When we spend more resources than we deposit, our body runs on a deficit, which can manifest as tiredness, irritability, or emotional discomfort. If the body budget's deficit is not corrected by deposits, the body goes "bankrupt," which can take the form of chronic illness, depression, or even death.

The more we deposit into our body budget, the more savings we accumulate. These savings then help us cover the everyday metabolic expenses without running into a deficit. For example, if you have a demanding job, make sure you are also prioritizing rest so your body and mind can recharge and maintain the energy needed to perform at your best. If you're fighting a common cold, instead of pushing through it, allow yourself to rest, prioritize hydration and proper nutrition, and use gentle movement to support your body in its recovery. When you learn something new, which can be very expensive on the body, make sure to refuel your body with adequate sleep, nutrition, and water, use physical activity, and take regular breaks to sustain your body budget.

Knowing we can support our body budget by intentionally making deposits through sleep, relaxation, movement, nutrients, and water, or by being in the presence of safe and supportive people, is very important knowledge for us to have, especially in challenging situations. Sometimes, in very difficult circumstances, such as the loss of a loved one, the metabolic expense might overpower the deposits we make, and we find ourselves experiencing longer periods of discomfort. So, during those times, it is even more important to continue making deposits to the body budget to modulate the intensity of the discomfort.

Our brain predicts our immediate future

The brain's way of coordinating the body budget is based on prediction. At any given moment, and without our conscious awareness, our brain is making predictions on what might happen in the immediate future, and it prepares the body to meet that prediction. More specifically, the brain coordinates the necessary changes such as the heart rate, intensity of breathing, contractions and movements of the muscles, or adjustments in hormone levels needed to prepare us for what we will see, hear, taste, smell, or feel. These predictions are made based on the sensory information we receive, the context we are in, and our memories of past experiences that resemble the current situation.

Let me give you an example of how this happens in real life. Imagine you are at a job interview and your brain is constantly making predictions about what might happen next. If you feel confident, your brain predicts a positive outcome—you might envision yourself answering questions clearly, engaging well with the interviewer, and leaving with a sense of accomplishment. As a result, your body might feel calm, poised, or even energized, which enhances your performance. However, if you feel insecure and nervous, your brain might predict that the interview will go poorly—perhaps you'll anticipate difficulty understanding or answering the questions clearly, making mistakes, or not being liked by the interviewer. These predictions can prompt a stress response, causing you to experience physical symptoms, like a racing heart, shaky hands, or difficulty focusing. Consequently, these physical manifestations of anxiety will weaken your performance. In both cases, your brain's predictions shape your behavior and, ultimately, influence the outcome—either positively or negatively. If you succeed after predicting a positive outcome, you're more likely to expect success next time, whereas if you fail after predicting the worst, you are more likely to anticipate failure again, reinforcing the cycle. But what happens when we make a prediction error, meaning that the prediction is inaccurate, and there's a mismatch between what the brain predicted and what actually ends up happening? Well, in that case, the brain updates itself by incorporating the new experience in future predictions. The popular name for this update is **learning**.

Let me use the job interview example to illustrate how this works. If you predicted success but struggled during the interview—that is, you made a prediction error—you may realize that while you felt confident going in, certain questions caught you off guard. To correct this, you might practice responses to a wider range of questions in the future to better prepare yourself for unexpected scenarios. The same applies if you predicted failure but performed well—also a prediction error. In this case, your worries might have led you to expect a bad outcome, but the interview went better than anticipated. So, in the future, you might recognize that your predictions could be driven by stress rather than evidence, and this awareness could help you to approach future interviews with more confidence. In both scenarios, you learned from the experience, and the likelihood of your brain creating more accurate predictions in the future increases.

So, are there any benefits to making accurate predictions? The answer is yes! Accurate predictions of the immediate future are less expensive for the body than prediction errors, because the brain operates more efficiently when it can anticipate outcomes with confidence. When the brain correctly predicts what will happen next, it doesn't have to expend as much energy processing surprises, stress responses, or uncertainties. Instead, the body is prepared for what is expected, and both the brain and body function smoothly without being overloaded.

On the other hand, situations where what actually happens differs from what we anticipated require more mental and physical energy because the brain has to work harder to resolve the discrepancy, reassess the situation, and adapt. This is an effort that can trigger stress responses, activate additional areas of the brain involved in problem-solving, and cause physiological reactions like increased heart rate or blood pressure. The brain and body are now engaged in correction, which consumes additional internal resources.

Although it is metabolically expensive to correct prediction errors—meaning, to learn from the experience—it is even more costly to continue making the same prediction errors, which happens when we fail to incorporate new information. In the job interview example, imagine you initially predicted failure, and this led to a poor performance. However, the poor performance was not because you didn't know the answers to the questions or because the interviewer didn't like you, but rather because your nervousness affected your ability to focus. Correcting this prediction error would involve acknowledging that the interview was not as bad as expected and using that insight to adjust your mindset for future interviews. This process of learning from the experience is metabolically expensive because it requires mental effort to reassess the situation, change your thought patterns, and implement new strategies for future situations. However, if you continue to predict failure in every interview without incorporating the information that interviews can be easier than expected, you end up repeating the same negative predictions.

Failure to adjust predictions that reflect new information becomes even more metabolically expensive over time because the brain will constantly use its energy to deal with stress, worry, and self-doubt, without making any progress toward a more accurate and adaptive expectation. Over time, the cycle of unaddressed prediction errors creates ongoing mental and physical strain, as the brain never learns from experiences and continues to operate based on outdated or inaccurate assumptions.

Emotional granularity

The brain uses concepts and categories as tools for prediction. The information they contain helps the brain make sense of what is happening inside and outside of the body so it can make accurate predictions. For example, the brain uses the concept of an emotion to understand and categorize internal experiences. We can categorize an emotional experience, ranging from very broad (like feeling bad, good, happy, or sad) to very specific (such as feeling pressured, playful, powerless, or respected). Broad categories carry less information than specific ones, and the broader the category the less information it carries. For example, feeling "bad" only tells us that we are experiencing an unpleasant emotion; it doesn't specify whether we feel sad, tired, or guilty. Even sadness, although it is more specific than feeling "bad," can hold various emotional states such as grief, regret, disappointment, or melancholy.

We develop emotional categories very early in life, within the context of our family and culture, and we continue to develop them throughout our lifetime. We learn through our experiences that the same internal sensation and situations can take different emotional meanings in different contexts. For example, lying on the beach can become happiness when we are on vacation, but it can be a source of guilt if we miss a work deadline because of it.

Similarly, a sensation in the stomach might indicate worry, insecurity, or deep feelings of affection toward someone, and a pounding heart might mean excitement, anger, or anticipation.

This nuanced differentiation between emotional experiences is called **emotional granularity**, and it plays an essential role in our wellbeing because it helps the brain make more accurate predictions and, consequently, coordinate more appropriate actions, which is metabolically beneficial for our body. The higher our emotional granularity—as in, the more specific we are in identifying and differentiating among various emotional states—the better our ability to assign accurate meaning to our internal states in any given situation. By accurately distinguishing between subtle variations of emotions with precision and detail, we reduce the metabolic expenses of our body budget.

CHAPTER 4

The Predictive Brain and Attachment

"The most critical discovery of recent decades in the field of neuroscience is that brain development is 'experience dependent.'"

Dr. Alan Sroufe

Why do our early years weigh so heavily in shaping the trajectory of our lives? The answer lies in the predictive nature of our brain. From the day we are born, our brain starts to pick up patterns and form predictions based on our primary caregivers' responses. As infants, we experience the world through our senses, and the primary caregivers' responses to us begin to structure those raw sensations into concepts and categories, which are then used to make predictions. That's how we learn how the world works and what to expect from others.

However, there is another key element to this story: the repetitiveness of these experiences. During our first years of life, we exist almost entirely in the presence of our primary caregivers, and by the time we enter other environments, our brain already has a bank of experiences to make predictions from. So if, during our first years, our primary caregivers were consistent in their care and support, our brain will continue to use that pattern of consistency and develop a coherent view of the world, which is the hallmark of secure attachment. On the other hand, when a person's early years are marked by ongoing uncertainty, their brain lacks the coherence needed to navigate the world accurately and efficiently, which characterizes insecure attachment.

In this chapter you will learn how the brain's predictive nature interacts with the early caregiving environment to construct the mental concepts that underlie attachment. And you will also gain an understanding of why the repetitive interactions with their caregivers shape one's view of the world— the very architecture of perception.

I will use Emma's story to illustrate how early childhood experiences shape people's internal model of the world. Emma was born into a family that believed children should respect parents by showing them appreciation for all the efforts they put into raising them. Her mother would openly talk about how difficult Emma was as a child and how demanding it was bringing her up. She would describe Emma as being a needy baby who used crying as manipulation. She believed that if Emma was fed and changed, there was no reason for her to cry. She even took pride in managing to resist Emma's use of "crying as manipulation" to be picked up from her crib. Emma's mother believed that parents who were responsive to their babies' cries were spoiling their babies and being manipulated by them. She openly criticized the parents who would jump to pick their babies up at any sign of discomfort or those who would hold them for long periods of time. She believed babies needed to be trained to fall asleep on their own by letting them cry in their cribs until they fell asleep. In her opinion, those parents who held their babies and cuddled them to sleep were weak and would end up regretting not training their babies to fall asleep on their own from the very beginning of their life, just as she had with Emma.

Emma's crying, just like any baby's crying, was a signal of discomfort and need for regulation from her mother. Emma's mother was responsive to her crying when she thought Emma was hungry or needed to be changed. However, in all other instances, she believed it was a sign of manipulation to gain attention and be picked up; therefore, she actively ignored Emma to avoid spoiling her. As a consequence, Emma would have intense episodes of crying spells that would end either when she fell asleep, exhausted from all the crying, or when her mother would become so irritated and tired of hearing Emma's crying, she would finally pick her up. Both scenarios reinforced the mother's belief that Emma used crying to manipulate her, and she needed to leave her crying in order to train her to sleep on her own.

Besides not "spoiling" Emma as a baby by holding and rocking her when crying, Emma's mother took good care of Emma. She was fed and changed appropriately and always dressed in cute little outfits that her mother would carefully choose for her. Emma was deeply loved by her mother, even though she considered Emma to be "too sensitive."

Unfortunately, Emma's mother's inconsistent responsiveness to her daughter's signs of distress created a sense of confusion in Emma very early in her childhood. This inconsistency in care created for Emma an internal model of the world in which her needs were sometimes responded to, while other times they were completely ignored. Her little brain wasn't provided with enough consistency to predict her mother's responses, which was very metabolically expensive for Emma's body budget.

Emma's concept of the world, created through her inconsistent early interactions with her mother, was that the world was unpredictable and, therefore, scary to venture into. As a young child, Emma preferred to spend time with her mother and would cling to her in situations when she needed to be left in the care of others, including her father. Her mother didn't mind spending time with Emma because she loved her very much, but she believed Emma was too clingy and demanding of her, which made her mother very upset at times and critical of Emma's "sensitivity." She wanted Emma to be more independent and less distressed when she wasn't around her.

When Emma started going to school, she soon found protection from the unpredictable world through her teacher. She really liked her teacher and was always eager to please her, soon becoming known as the teacher's "helper." She didn't spend much time with other children, but there was one group of girls she liked and would sometimes follow around. When they chose to play with other children, Emma would become really upset and accuse them of being mean, which made them not want to be around her sometimes. These experiences further reinforced Emma's predictions that the world is inconsistent and unpredictable. Over time, she found a best friend who she admired, followed, and copied in almost everything she did. They were best friends until their teenage years, when their relationship became distant due to going to different high schools, which was devastating for Emma at the time. During high school, Emma made new friends, but her relationships weren't consistent. Most of the time, she felt betrayed by her friends, which further reinforced her predictions that she couldn't rely on others and created many moments of deep suffering for her. Despite her efforts to please others, she felt like she was never enough for them. Emma's first romantic relationship also ended up with betrayal, which left Emma in a state of depression. With each new relationship, she became more and more anxious to express her needs out of fear she would be left by her partners. In her mid-20s, after a few failed relationships, numerous anxiety attacks, and states of depression, she decided to seek psychotherapy. With the help of her therapist, she was able to create a more coherent and accurate narrative of her experiences. During the therapeutic process, Emma also learned how to create new and secure relationships, which expanded her view of the world and, as a consequence, changed her life trajectory toward more security.

The neural foundation of attachment

For better or worse, the way we see and interact with the world is shaped by our early caregiving environment. We are born with a brain that is still developing, ready to be wired to its environment. Every smell, sound, or touch, each moment of comfort or discomfort leaves a physical mark on our brain in the form of a neural connection. Each repetitive interaction with the environment, or lack of it, strengthens the neural connections in the brain reflecting that interaction, and it creates the foundation for how we see and interact with the world.

Because we enter the world with an undeveloped brain and body, we are completely dependent on others for survival. We are constantly bombarded by raw and undefined sensory inputs, without yet having mental representations of those sensory experiences. Over time, the brain starts to detect and predict sensory patterns, which leads to the gradual creation of mental concepts and categories. For example, an initial undefined visual input becomes the concept of a face, which then becomes the concept of a mother, which can then be placed in various categories, such as reliable, unreliable, comforting, or scary. These concepts and categories are shaped by the individual differences in maternal care and the unique environment we develop within.

Over time, the brain assembles these categories and develops predictive models that support the regulation of the body. Before that happens, the regulation of an infant's body budget takes place through the biological and behavioral synchrony between the infant and the mother. For example, the mother regulates the infant's body temperature by holding the baby close to her body, their immune system through breastfeeding, and their level of arousal through a soft and gentle tone of voice. Even their heart rate is regulated by the mother, which can have significant implications on the infant when the mother's heart rate is increased due to her own dysregulation. Over time, this synchrony between the mother and the infant supports the infant in becoming a person who can regulate their own body budget and even support the regulation of others.

Growing a brain that can appropriately coordinate the complex systems of our body budget requires care from a sensitively attuned and consistently responsive caregiver, which enables the infant's brain to develop structures that help detect regularities in the environment. These regularities then help the infant predict the sensory input provided by the caregiver, which is beneficial for the infant's body budget. For example, the mother's smell starts to be associated with food, her voice with comfort, and her gentle touch with rest.

A sensitively attuned mother regulates her infant's body budget by responding to the infant's cues of dysregulation, such as crying. When the mother and the infant are in synchrony, the infant is not only kept alive but thrives. This synchrony creates the infant's neuronal foundation for secure attachment. In contrast, when this synchrony is disrupted, and as a consequence the regulation of the body budget is obstructed, the neural foundation of the infant's brain is wired for an insecure attachment.

There are various factors that might disrupt the biobehavioral synchrony between the infant and their mother. A baby might be born prematurely and placed under continuous medical observation without parental access. A child might become an orphan and suddenly be faced with multiple changes to their environment. A mother might experience postpartum depression that interferes with her capacity to connect with and respond to the infant's needs. A primary caregiver with an insecure attachment style might react to the infant's cues of dysregulation by exaggerating their needs, which can further dysregulate the infant, or by minimizing or ignoring them, leaving the infant's needs unattended. A primary caregiver may struggle with their own regulation and lack the ability to attune sensitively to the infant's needs. Drug use or mental illness may be present, increasing the caregiver's irritability and aggression and decreasing their capacity to attune and tend to the infant's needs. The primary caregiver might be a single parent with no support from their community, which can be extremely tiring and taxing on their wellbeing, consequently impacting the infant. A primary caregiver could have daily periods of absence due to work demands, illness, or other responsibilities that disrupts the infant–caregiver synchrony.

All the above real-life scenarios could affect the way the infant's brain develops and have long-lasting consequences. Inconsistency in care, for example, creates irregularity in sensory input coming from the environment. When this happens, the little brain cannot create accurate predictions, which can be very metabolically expensive. As a result, that little brain creates an internal model of an inconsistent and unreliable world. On the other hand, when an infant is faced with neglect, meaning there is no response to their crying, and therefore their needs go unattended, they learn that the world is unresponsive. Moreover, when the infant's crying is met with impatience, irritability, aggression, or abuse, the little brain learns that the world is threatening and unsafe. In all these scenarios, not only does the infant's body budget go unattended by the caregiver, but it is also very metabolically taxing for the infant.

All early experiences, pleasant and unpleasant, become foundational concepts that shape our internal model of the world, and future predictions are then made based on this model. With each new accurate prediction, this view of the world is strengthened, which results in more similar predictions in the future. New experiences of safety and consistency can help the brain expand its model of the world as a safe and predictable place and, as a consequence, create new predictions of safety. However, in the case of severe abuse or neglect, the brain will continue to weigh those experiences very heavily in future predictions, because missing a threat would be far more taxing for the body budget than predicting it. These predictions help the brain prepare the body to deal with the adversities of the environment. Over time, this continuous preparation of the body to deal with adversity becomes a burden on the metabolic body budget, and it creates long-lasting consequences for the person's physiological, psychological, and relational wellbeing.

Repetitive experiences develop attachment patterns

The key element that creates the neuronal foundation of a secure or insecure attachment is the repetitiveness of similar experiences. Since our first years of life are limited to the experiences provided by our primary caregivers, our brains are shaped solely based on these experiences. During our formative early years, our interactions are largely limited to those with our caregivers. Their ways of interacting with us, their rules and values, or the absence of them, shape our internal view of the world. By the time we have access to other environments, such as school, we already have strong neuronal systems that we base our predictions on. This is why our early experiences weigh so heavily on how we see and interact with the world.

The nature of the child's attachment is not a reflection of the parent's love for the child. Rather, it is the parent's own attachment style and stressors that impact their interaction with the child. For example, a parent with an unexamined dismissive attachment style is likely to become irritated and even angry with their child's expression of discomfort—not because they don't love the child; the struggle lies in their own inability to tolerate the child's discomfort. The child's discomfort brings to the surface the parent's own vulnerabilities that were never acknowledged or tended to, and for that reason, they don't have a model of how to soothe themself or the child in times of distress. Their own way to manage discomfort is either by dismissing it or forcefully suppressing it. In real life, that could look like completely ignoring the child's crying or by responding to it in a threatening way. These reactions can be verbal or nonverbal and range from mild to more intense forms. For example, mild verbal responses could sound like, "Stop crying, it's not a big deal," "What's wrong with you?" "Why are you crying right now?" "Stop being a crybaby," "You are too sensitive." Whereas more intense reactions might sound like, "If you don't stop crying, I will give you something to cry about," "You are a bad child," "You are the worst child," "You ruined my life," "I wish you were never born," "I hate you," "Everyone hates you." On the other hand, nonverbal messages could range from completely ignoring the child, walking away, eye-rolling, expressions of contempt, clenching fists, loud clapping to get attention, throwing or slamming objects.

These are all real-life examples of parents who love their children but don't have the capacity to sensitively attune to their children's needs in times of distress or respond to those needs with empathy and compassion. These parents are not bad people who hate their children; it's quite the opposite—they are likely to experience deep discomfort and feelings of shame during and after those situations. Oftentimes, after they calm down, they might even apologize to the child or make loving gestures toward them to make up for their abrasive reactions. Unfortunately, if these situations repeat over and over again, for months and years, the child learns that to avoid criticism, anger, or even physical violence, they must hide their needs in times of discomfort. So, to avoid their parent's harsh responses, the child learns to suppress their distress, withdraw in difficult times, and not ask for help when they need it. They also learn that they are only worthy of their parent's love and affection when they don't show any signs of distress.

By the time the child enters other environments, they already have an internal model of the world based on which they predict that vulnerability is either ignored or responded to with disapproval, frustration, and sometimes with physical harm. To avoid these insensitive reactions, the child might avoid others, withdraw when feeling vulnerable, or hide their vulnerability by responding with aggression. These ways of interacting with others then create further situations that strengthen the person's belief that they need to hide their vulnerability and discomfort in order to avoid negative reactions.

CHAPTER 5

Attachment Is Stable but Not Fixed

"We are architects of our own experience."

Dr. Lisa Feldman Barrett

Will the shadows of our early childhood experiences always haunt us? Well… it depends. Although there is a great deal of stability in the attachment styles, change can happen, both intentionally and unintentionally. There are various changes in our circumstances that can have a significant impact on our sense of security which, consequently, would impact the trajectory of our life. That is to say, developing early attachment security is not a guarantee of becoming a securely attached adult—just like having an insecure attachment style doesn't mean you can never earn security in close relationships.

In this chapter, I intend to bring hope to those with a history of insecure attachment. I will draw upon scientific evidence, as well as lived experiences, to show you there is a path from insecure attachment to earned security. Although this path can be uncomfortable and even discouraging at times, it is worth the effort. Thankfully, we live in a time with easy access to information and a variety of very effective therapeutic programs that we can go through to process and heal old attachment wounds.

One thing is for sure: you don't have to stay stuck in the predicament of your childhood. Having an insecure attachment is not your fault, but changing it is your responsibility. There are intentional choices and behaviors that can earn you security—an end goal that we should all strive for.

The most successful story of earned security I have ever witnessed belongs to Maya. I met Maya in her mid-20s, when she was actively working on… living a good life. Maya was at the beginning of her career as a psychotherapist, deeply immersed in the science of attachment. With each new piece of information, she dove deeper into reflecting on her own attachment style just to discover she had a fearful-avoidant attachment style. This discovery came with deep and difficult feelings of sadness for all she'd had to endure as a child. She also felt anger for experiencing fear inflicted by her parents, the very people who were supposed to love her, and who indeed loved her deeply. She felt sorrow for all the times she had been confused or terrified by her parents' behavior.

Maya was fully engaged in her journey of processing early childhood memories and the associated feelings, and she was not shying away from it. The reason she was going full force into processing her history of insecure attachment, despite the deep discomfort that came with it, was the promise of an earned security. While she was learning about her own attachment style, she was also learning about the benefits of having a secure attachment. Maya wanted so badly to experience the benefits of a secure attachment that she was willing to do whatever it took to get there, including revisiting painful childhood memories.

As she was processing these memories, she was also developing a new, more coherent narrative of her life. This included both the bad and good news of her childhood; Maya revisited feelings and situations without minimizing or exaggerating them. She struggled the most with allowing the bad news of her childhood to be as bad as it was while maintaining a loving relationship with her parents. There were times when she wasn't sure it would be possible for her to have a close relationship with her parents or whether she could have a life without chaos in it.

During this process of self-reflection, Maya was also dating, with the hope of marriage and children. After a couple of short-lived relationships in which she was able to identify and name her insecure pattern of attachment, she met a young man she fell in love with and they started planning a life together. It was during this relationship that she implemented all the strategies that were promised to help her earn security in the relationship. She did everything under the sun: therapy, journaling, meditation, patterns of deep breathing, self-compassion, and more. In times of distress, she even started asking for help and support from her partner and other people she trusted. She began to overtly communicate her needs and desires instead of doing it subtly or hoping that others could read her mind. Maya was on a mission to create security in her relationship.

Unfortunately, this young man's family were completely opposed to him marrying outside of their culture. Although he loved Maya, he felt he couldn't go against his family's wishes, which brought uncertainty into their relationship. This was a pivotal moment for Maya. She needed to make a conscious decision whether to leave him and continue pursuing her dream of building a family or stay in the relationship, where she felt loved by him but the prospect of marriage and children was uncertain. They genuinely loved each other, and there was a possibility the relationship could lead to marriage, but the uncertainty of the situation was too much for Maya to bear. It was tapping into her insecure attachment and taking its toll on her, a toll she wasn't willing to pay anymore. She knew she had to break up with him if she wanted security. As hard as it was for her to walk away from the relationship, and as much as they both suffered for a while, she was determined to find a man who wanted to commit and build a family with her. A few months after the breakup, she met her current husband, with whom she built a secure relationship. As I write this, a decade later, Maya is living a good life with her husband and their daughter.

The unknown that Maya encountered throughout her journey toward earned security felt overwhelming at times, stirring up fears of all the things that could go wrong, leaving her vulnerable. During those times, she had to put her trust in the information she was learning from science, implement the self-regulation strategies she picked up along the way, and seek help from the secure people around her who were gently supporting her through those difficult times.

Earned security

Maya's story of earned security demonstrates that we do not have to be trapped in the predicament of an insecure attachment style. There is ample scientific evidence showing that, with new experiences in which security and coherence are nurtured, transformation is possible at any age. To this day, one of the longest studies on attachment, The Minnesota Longitudinal Study of Parents and Children, continues to provide us with valuable information about the influencing factors that can make one's world become more secure and coherent.

The Minnesota study started over 50 years ago when a group of scientists decided to follow a cohort of people and their newly born babies with the intention to investigate and understand attachment development. Over the years, the scientists consistently observed the interactions between the children and their parents, as well as the children's interactions with others in settings such as schools and summer camps. Researchers also interviewed the children's parents, teachers, and other adults involved in the caregiving of the children, to gather information about the children's social, emotional, and behavioral functioning in those settings. As years passed, the researchers continued to follow these children and witness their development all the way into adulthood. The study is still active and continues to provide us with valuable information about the effects of early childhood environments on adulthood, the transmission of attachment styles from one generation to another, and how stable attachment styles are over time.

Results from the study show us that positive change can happen in a person's life when stressors decrease and social support increases. Say, if in childhood the parent of an insecure child undergoes a personal transformation—for example, by going to therapy or attaining sobriety—and becomes attuned and responsive to the child's needs, the child can develop security within that relationship. A supportive adult during childhood years, such as a family member, teacher, or coach, might also be able to break the predicament of an insecure attachment style by providing the child with the experience of safety and security in their relationship.

In adulthood, however, change is primarily contingent on us—we need to take active steps that lead to security. For example, choosing a securely attached partner who is supportive and nurturing can positively influence our sense of security. Deciding to seek professional support could also play a significant role in positive change, since remarkable transformation can happen through psychotherapy. The point is, throughout our life, we can take intentional steps to create attachment security within our close relationships. Earning security is not an easy path for those with an insecure attachment, but perpetuating the patterns of the insecure attachment is an even harder one.

We can create new predictions

The childhood experiences that led to the development of insecure attachment don't have to dominate our existence. As Maya's story shows, although the memories of our past influence our present, we do not have to be trapped in our early childhood experiences. We can't erase the past, but we can build new memories that expand the way we perceive the world. How can we do that? By exposing ourselves to new experiences. With intention, we can create new experiences that add to our brain's flexibility to predict differently in the future. Every new piece of information we learn through new and pleasant experiences becomes a memory, which the brain uses to predict differently tomorrow. We can also develop new strategies that help us manage the content of our past experiences and our physiological reactions to them.

Having awareness that our past experiences are continuously shaping our present is key. This awareness can significantly influence the various decisions we make to support our physiological and psychological balance. If we want to change our life's trajectory toward more security, we need to change our brain's predictions, because that's what constructs the experience of our body in the world. Put simply, we can become the architects of our own experiences.

Who we choose matters

Attachment security is key to connection. We cannot have meaningful close relationships if we don't feel secure in those relationships. The bad news is that the core feature of the insecure attachment styles is a lack of safety and security in close relationships. This is why people with insecure attachments often end up in unfulfilling relationships filled with uncertainty, stress, and difficult moments. However, the good news is we can intentionally choose to enter relationships with people who can provide us with the stability and safety of a secure relationship. What's more, we can choose to end relationships in which we feel insecure and that bring a great deal of stress into our lives. In other words, looking for security is equally important as avoiding insecure situations.

Securely attached people can provide the positive support and interactions that someone with an insecure attachment needs in a relationship. Securely attached people do not become overwhelmed by distress, which helps them remain grounded in the present moment, regardless of the situation they are in. Even in difficult circumstances, they remain consistent in their behavior and maintain the belief that they are valued despite their imperfections. In essence, they see imperfections as part of being human. When things go wrong, they tend to turn to others with kindness rather than criticism and offer their support. For all these reasons, a securely attached person can be a source of comfort, safety, and predictability—all necessary ingredients for a secure relationship—for someone with an insecure attachment. The longer these positive interactions with a securely attached person last, the more likely it is for security to develop in the relationship.

Security within ourselves

Although it is important to choose wisely when deciding who to surround ourselves with (so we don't repeat the cycle of insecurity), developing a sense of security doesn't always have to be contingent on others. We can also develop a sense of security within our own selves. How we see and interact with our own self matters just as much as how we see and interact with others. Examining our perception of self is key in the process of developing internal security, since this perception influences our internal dialogue and behavior.

Our self-concept is developed based on the repetitive messages we received from our caregivers. The way we perceive ourselves is a mirror of how our caregivers perceived us when we were growing up. If the feedback received from our caregivers was consistently caring and loving, our internal view of self will also be caring and loving. In contrast, if the feedback received from our caregivers was consistently harsh and critical, our internal view of self will also be harsh and critical. Our caregivers' responses to us, especially in times of distress, created a profound and long-lasting impact on our sense of self, and having awareness of how our early experiences shaped our perception of self is essential for developing a more accurate and positive self-perception.

We all have limitations, and being faced with them can create various levels of distress in us. However, how we respond to these limitations matters greatly because it can help us soothe our distress or deepen it further, thus creating suffering. When we approach our distress with loving care, kindness, and compassion, we are actively soothing the discomfort we are experiencing. Loving care might take the form of seeking the company of our loved ones, asking for help when needed, allowing ourselves to rest, or eating nutritious food to support the optimal functioning of our body. Kindness and compassion amid a difficult experience can be in the form of loving self-talk and having a non-judgmental attitude while acknowledging that difficulties are part of life. This approach supports our ability to navigate challenges without being overwhelmed by them. Additionally, it creates a sense of trust in ourselves, knowing we can access internal resources that could help us face and go through difficulties.

In contrast, when we meet our limitations with criticism and self-judgment, we are adding an unnecessary burden on ourselves, which creates suffering. This added emotional load strains our capacity to navigate difficulties effectively and creates more experiences that deepen our belief that we are inadequate. This harsh approach further cultivates a negative internal dialogue, perpetuating our suffering and undermining our ability to learn and grow from our experiences. Simply put, we not only suppress our growth, but we also become our own source of pain, creating a cycle in which we are the abuser and the abused at the same time. Awareness of this self-defeating cycle is key in breaking free from it; however, it is only the first step toward cultivating more security within us. What we additionally need is to embrace a kinder and more self-compassionate internal dialogue, especially in times of distress, to foster a more supportive relationship with ourselves and, as a result, create more internal security.

CHAPTER 6

Early Attachment and Shame

"Shame is a soul eating emotion."

Dr. Carl Jung

Our earliest relationships shape the way we experience shame—how we feel about ourselves, how we react to failure, and how we carry the weight of imperfection through life. Shame is a complex and powerful emotion that stems from the belief that we are inadequate, unworthy, or fundamentally flawed. Unlike guilt, which arises from the belief that we have done something wrong, shame is rooted in the belief that there is something inherently wrong with us.

Shame often develops during our early childhood interactions with our parents and other important people around us. The quality of these interactions and the messages we receive, both positive and negative, shape the frequency and intensity of our experience with shame. There are various degrees of shame we can experience, from everyday embarrassment to shame proneness—the first one being situational and short lasting, while the other is a frequent and intense experience of inadequacy that lingers for a longer time, deeply affecting our sense of self-worth.

The seeds of shame are planted in our early attachment, shaping our sense of worth and our inner dialogue. Those with secure attachment are more likely to develop an inner voice that is supportive and compassionate, while those with insecure attachment are likely to have an inner dialogue marked by self-judgment and shame. The purpose of this chapter is to explore the complex nature of shame, examine its distinction from guilt and everyday embarrassment, and highlight how early attachment influences the development of our internal narrative.

Emotions are part of my work, just as numbers are for an accountant. No day passes by without me thinking and talking about emotions in some way or another. I approach every emotion with curiosity—whether that is joy, sadness, anger, fear, or anything in between— genuinely interested in the information they carry. Acknowledging and accurately identifying our emotions is important because they can help us navigate life with more ease, connect more deeply with others and understand our needs more clearly. They can even help protect us from harm.

Among them all, there is one particular emotion whose power continues to puzzle me due to its intricate layers, and that is shame. There is no other emotion quite like it—a hidden force, present but easily mistaken for something else. Shame is a uniquely elusive emotion, constantly shifting its form and expression, making it difficult to recognize. Its ability to masquerade as other emotions such as anger, sadness, or even indifference makes it all the more powerful because it can hide in plain sight, slipping unnoticed into every part of our existence.

Shame is an aspect of the human story, meaning that we all experience it in various degrees and with varying frequency. I've never encountered a person who has never experienced shame, but I have met many who were not aware of their shame because it was either mistaken as a different emotion— such as anger, sadness, contempt, jealousy, envy, worry, loneliness, fear—or was masked by humor, perfectionism, or indifference. *How can shame be so tricky?* you might wonder. Why is it so difficult to recognize? Well, although the process is complex, the answer is quite simple: to protect one's own *self*, as it would when under attack. Let me explain…

Shame makes us feel unworthy and exposed—a deeply uncomfortable, vulnerable, and isolating experience. The pain of shame can be so overwhelming that our minds need to create protective strategies to shield us from it, helping us avoid or minimize the distress it causes. Those strategies are not conscious nor used with intention. They are unconscious and automatic, meaning we are not aware of them unless we actively reflect on our experiences. It often takes a lot of self-awareness, introspection, or psychotherapy to recognize these unconscious defenses against shame and work through them.

Acknowledging shame is not an easy thing to do, because it involves acknowledging vulnerabilities such as helplessness, humiliation, or being negatively judged by others—all threats to our sense of *self*. Admitting helplessness, for instance, feels like admitting a lack of control over our own circumstances, which can be terrifying. Humiliation, on the other hand, hits at our core sense of self-worth, striking at the heart of who we believe ourselves to be. So, acknowledging humiliation means facing the possibility that we might be seen as inadequate, flawed, or inferior in some way, which is a direct threat to our dignity and worth. If we admit the negative judgment of others, we have to accept that we are not measuring up to their expectations and might be seen as a failure.

The possibility of being exposed to such harsh judgment and sitting with the unbearable discomfort can lead us to deflect with anger, avoidance, or even by distracting ourselves with superficial concerns to protect ourselves. These unconscious protective strategies may create some temporary relief by offering a sense of control in moments where we would otherwise feel exposed and weak. However, in the long run, they prevent us from acknowledging, processing, and healing deep-rooted wounds.

The greatest challenge with shame is not that it is the most excruciating of emotions but that it often goes unrecognized when we experience it. When we fail to recognize shame for what it is—an emotion that stems from a fear of being exposed as being fundamentally flawed—we can experience a variety of negative outcomes, such as misguided reactions, isolation, or anger, all affecting our relationship with both the self and others. For example, imagine you are feeling ashamed about not being able to meet your partner's expectations, but instead of recognizing it as shame, you start to act irritated or distant, which might be interpreted as a lack of care by your partner, leading to resentment in the relationship. Instead, if you're able to recognize shame, your reactions would not be irritation and distance but rather self-compassion for experiencing such a painful emotion.

Let's take another example, one that involves perfectionism. If you are a highly successful individual, always striving to be the best at everything you do, on the surface it can look like you are just exceptionally dedicated and hardworking, when, truly, your perfectionism could be rooted in shame. It might be the fear of being imperfect or "not enough" that drives your need to be flawless, constantly proving your value to yourself and others by being "right" or perfect. There is nothing wrong with striving for excellence, but if this drive is rooted in shame, any small setback has the potential to become devastating, and every minor criticism might be interpreted as a reflection of unworthiness.

Other examples can include fear of not fitting in or not being "good enough" socially, so you might avoid situations where you could feel judged, hindering your opportunities to develop relationships or grow professionally. You might even label yourself as antisocial, introverted, or awkward, completely unaware that what you are protecting yourself from is shame. This misinterpretation can further isolate you, creating a feedback loop where shame grows stronger, and the cycle of isolation becomes harder to break.

You might also protect yourself from the excruciating pain of shame by focusing on others. For example, you might tend to constantly judge or criticize people's choices or lifestyle, often competing with others, even in small or insignificant ways, continuously striving to outperform and outshine them, or acting superior to position yourself as "better than" them. Diverting attention from self to others might provide you with a temporary distraction from the internal emotional turmoil stemming from shame, but in the long term it perpetuates feelings of insecurity and resentment, eventually leading to patterns of envy and jealousy. So while focusing outward may temporarily mask the discomfort of shame, it prevents you from genuine healing—instead of addressing the shame with kindness and care, you remain stuck in a cycle of avoidance.

There are endless examples of how shame can negatively impact our lives when we are not aware of it. If we want to reduce its impact, we need to know what shame is, how it develops, and how it manifests in our lives. So, let's learn more about shame.

What is shame?

The experience of shame is part of being human, and it stems from beliefs such as *I am not good enough, Something is innately wrong with me*, or *I am defective*. It is a painful emotion that leads us to perceive ourselves as being fundamentally flawed, unworthy, or somehow broken. This perception leads to a negative view of ourselves and can leave us feeling diminished, inadequate, unimportant, invisible, alone, and not valued. There are situations in which we experience feelings of shame, ranging from moments of painful embarrassment to excruciating feelings of worthlessness.

Shame vs guilt

While the feeling of shame stems from the belief that ***I am*** *wrong*, the feeling of guilt is rooted in the belief that ***I did*** *something wrong*. Although both are unpleasant experiences, they differ significantly from each other. For example, I could feel embarrassed about *doing* something wrong; however, the very fact that I can do something about it is what differentiates guilt from shame. When I am *doing* something wrong, I can take actions to apologize for my wrongdoing, and in some cases even remediate the situation. In contrast, if my belief is that *something is wrong with me*, there is nothing I can do about it, and it is likely I would try my best to hide that part of myself that I perceive as being inherently wrong. Put another way, while guilt tells me that *I did* something wrong and I might be able to fix it, shame tells me that *I am* wrong, innately defective, and therefore there is nothing I can do about it.

Everyday embarrassment vs shame-proneness

Day-to-day embarrassment is something we all face at times. Who among us hasn't experienced situations in which our limitations or shortcomings were exposed? Perhaps you've been called out in front of your peers, been laughed at when sharing an idea, were caught telling a lie, or been in any other situation in which you felt like your face had caught on fire and you wished you could vanish in that very moment. Although unpleasant, it is something we can recover from without lasting consequences, besides a brief shiver that comes with the memory of the situation.

In contrast, people who are shame-prone carry a profound sensitivity to perceived judgment or rejection and are likely to experience deep and persistent feelings of shame. For someone who is shame-prone, the propensity to feel shame can be so intense that even neutral or well-meaning comments might feel like personal attacks. The slightest sign that someone *might* be giving them feedback can feel threatening; it is not about the feedback itself but the anticipation of it. No matter how kind or constructive the remarks, their mind jumps ahead and prepares for emotional pain because any input feels like a threat to their worth. Why? Because in past experiences, comments were tied to shame, punishment, or abandonment. So even neutral feedback cues like "Hey, can I talk to you about something?" or "I just wanted to mention something I noticed" can instantly put them on edge and activate a self-defeating inner dialogue, such as *What did I do wrong?, They probably think I'm a failure,* or *I knew I wasn't good enough.*

Even a kind-hearted joke could feel like confirmation that they are inadequate and unlovable. The same applies with teasing comments—they might be interpreted as criticism or mockery, even when there's no intention to hurt. This happens because shame-prone individuals tend to receive them as reflections of who *they* believe they are: inherently flawed and unworthy. This kind of sensitivity develops during early experiences—growing up in an environment where love and approval feel conditional, or where mistakes are met with harsh judgment or ridicule.

Insecure attachment: The root of shame

Shame is a learned emotion. Children learn this emotion through their caregivers' use of shaming messages, both verbal and nonverbal. When the caregiver consistently fails to respond to the child's needs, and instead reacts with distress, disappointment, criticism, anger, or contempt, the child's adaptive reaction is shame. When the caregiver uses shaming messages, the child feels judged as being "bad" or defective, ending up feeling diminished. Even as adults, those who recall their caregivers as being overprotective or rejecting are more likely to experience feelings of inadequacy and self-hate. On the other hand, those who remember their caregivers as being warm and caring tend to have a sense of compassionate regard toward their own self, especially when things go wrong.

Those with insecure attachments tend to carry with them the feelings of shame experienced during childhood into adult life. In contrast, those who are securely attached maintain the positive self-view formed during childhood, even in times of distress. So while insecurely attached people are likely to experience feelings of shame, those with secure attachment remain anchored in their belief that they are worthy despite their imperfections. Unlike people with insecure attachment, those who are securely attached can realistically assess both the positive and the more limited aspects of themselves, which helps them maintain a realistic self-view even when things go wrong.

As you can see, a person's basic sense of worth and value comes from the responsiveness of the primary caregiver to their needs. When the parent is sensitively attuned to the child and consistently responds to their needs with care and warmth, it validates the child's *self*. Without this validation, the child feels invisible, unworthy, and not valued. When ignored, a child feels unimportant, defective, and develops a negative view of self that is carried into adult life.

Early attachment develops our inner voice

The early messages we receive from our parents become our inner voice. This voice can be a reliable source of comfort, calmness, and safety, or it can be harsh, critical, and shaming. You may or may not be aware of your internal voice, and if you are, there is a fair chance you have never questioned its roots or development.

We develop an inner dialogue early on in our lives, based on the quality of our relationships with our parents. Children with secure attachment who are consistently responded to with warmth, kindness, and care internalize these responses and develop an internal dialogue they can rely on as a source of comfort during times of distress. In contrast, insecurely attached children who are responded to with criticism, anger, or rejection in times of distress internalize those interactions and develop a harsh critical internal dialogue. The harsher and more shaming the inner voice becomes, the more likely it is the person will experience intense feelings of being defective and unworthy.

This internal narrative we develop in childhood becomes ingrained in our sense of identity and carries into adulthood, shaping how we perceive ourselves and others and how we navigate life. The way parents spoke to us during our formative years influences whether our internal voice is kind and supportive or critical and diminishing. As we grow, this voice continues to subconsciously guide our decisions, emotions, and self-worth throughout our life.

When shame becomes our internal voice, it distorts our reality, making us focus on our flaws and mistakes rather than our strengths and potential, which often happens for people with insecure attachments. Over time, this negative inner narrative shapes our identity and how we relate to others, causing us to hide parts of ourselves, avoid vulnerability, and live in fear of judgment or rejection. Typically, people with insecure attachments fail to acknowledge that experiencing shame is part of being human, and they tend to either consistently worry about being judged or rejected or struggle to acknowledge their emotions at all, ending up suppressing them completely. They might focus on and overidentify with their limitations, view emotions as unacceptable and a sign of weakness; or struggle to make sense of their experience. In those situations, their degree of empathy and compassion toward themself and others is significantly diminished.

CHAPTER 7

The Power of Self-Compassion

"If your compassion does not include yourself, it is incomplete."

Jack Kornfield

What if the way we speak to ourselves could change everything? What if being kind to ourselves is how we move from holding it all together to finally feeling enough? What if acknowledging our limitations wasn't a sign of weakness but the very thing that could help us navigate life with clarity and trust?

We are often taught that being hard on ourselves is the path to growth—that if we just push harder, strive for more, and silence the "inner softness," we will finally become "enough." But constant self-criticism doesn't make us stronger. As a matter of fact, it wears us down. In contrast, self-compassion offers us a different way of relating to ourselves, one rooted in kindness and support instead of self-criticism and blame. This is not about ignoring our limitations or avoiding responsibility; it is about meeting ourselves with kindness *despite* the struggle or the belief that we are not good enough. It is about treating ourselves with the same care and understanding we would offer to someone we love.

This chapter is an invitation to explore what self-compassion truly is: not just a concept, but a practice we can return to again and again. We will also explore some common misconceptions that tend to get in the way, like the idea that self-compassion is selfish or makes us weak. Along the way, I will highlight the benefits of self-compassion to show that being kind to ourselves is not just something nice to do; it is a powerful influence on our wellbeing.

———————————

I discovered the concept of self-compassion more than a decade ago, and I started practicing it in the hope that my own personal experience would match the research findings—I had read various studies showing that increased levels of self-compassion were associated with positive outcomes such as better mental and physical health, increased motivation, higher levels of self-worth, and supportive relationships. It felt too good to be true, but the scientific evidence was speaking loud enough for me to listen. If being kind and loving toward myself could really increase my wellbeing, improve my relationships, make me trust myself more, and strengthen my motivation, there was no other road I would've rather taken. I was completely sold on it from the very beginning.

Starting a self-compassion practice wasn't something I knew how to do, but I was determined to figure it out so I could gain its benefits. I started with small steps, the first one being spending one minute mindfully observing my experience. Every morning, while sitting on the side of the bed and before taking my first step into the day, I took a minute to notice my experience— how my body felt, the quality of my thoughts, and what type of emotions I was feeling in that moment. Day after day, for a full minute, I was inviting my experience into my awareness without judgment and without dismissing, minimizing, or overidentifying with it. This daily minute of mindful noticing allowed me to witness various degrees of pleasant feelings, such as joy, excitement, contentment, hope, but also difficult feelings like fear, grief, shame, pain, and suffering. I savored the pleasant ones whenever they arose, and I allowed the unpleasant feelings the space to be seen, heard, and felt. Perhaps for the first time in my life, I didn't fight the uncomfortable feelings.

Over the period of a year, the one minute grew into five, ten, twenty, thirty, forty-five, sixty minutes of mindful noticing, ultimately transforming into mindful awareness throughout the day. This wasn't a linear or easy process, but the gained awareness of my daily experience was priceless. I witnessed the good and the bad days, and I became aware of my patterns of thoughts, feelings, and interactions. Some days were really pleasant and easy—I noticed the trees' vibrant shades of green, the vast blue sky, the chirping of the birds, the sound of crickets, the hopes and dreams I was creating, and my desire to connect with others.

Other days were really hard and difficult to bear—I felt fatigued, consumed with my own thoughts, and the world felt small and scary. Witnessing the effects of those difficult times on my body and my thoughts made me want to turn toward myself with love and care, just as I would toward a dear friend. The empathy and compassion I started feeling toward myself in difficult situations softened my heart and brought a sense of ease into those moments of suffering. There were days when I would allow myself to slow down, cry, or wrap myself in a blanket—all gestures of kindness, care, and support.

I was a little bit reluctant to embrace self-compassion at first. I was afraid I would develop a habit of allowing myself to be weak or self-indulgent. I was afraid I was encouraging self-pity. In the beginning, responding with love and kindness to my experiences, especially after a failed attempt at something I cared about, felt like free-falling. Even so, I persisted in my practice because I trusted the scientific evidence. Over time, with each self-compassionate response, I created a new experience of safety and care within myself. This newfound internal safety is now a source of information that my brain uses for predictions. Even in the most difficult times, I know I can rely on my practice of self-compassion to modulate the intensity and duration of my distress. Using the metaphor of the body budget, with each self-compassionate act, I am making a deposit in times of metabolically taxing situations. What started with one minute of observing my experience is now my way of being. Self-compassion is and will always be part of my experience. Flaws and all, in times of success or failure, I will always be on my side. The gentle voice of self-compassion will always whisper in my ear, "I love you, always."

What is self-compassion?

Self-compassion is the ability to acknowledge our distress when we are struggling and respond to it with kindness while recognizing that pain is part of the human experience. Meaning that instead of ignoring, minimizing, or exaggerating our experiences in difficult times, we acknowledge and respond to them with the intention of soothing the discomfort. A big part of having a self-compassionate attitude is recognizing that we, humans, are imperfect and, as a consequence, we are prone to making mistakes.

A self-compassionate state of mind grows from three nurturing roots: **mindfulness, self-kindness,** and **common humanity. Mindfulness** refers to our capacity to stay grounded in the present moment, aware of our body and mind in relationship with the environment, and open to our suffering in difficult times without judgment, denial, or suppression of whatever feelings, thoughts, or sensations may arise. The opposite of mindfulness is overidentification, which is the tendency to become consumed by unpleasant emotions, thoughts, and sensations that arise in challenging situations. Oftentimes, when we encounter difficult situations, we tend to dismiss unpleasant feelings and painful sensations or ruminate over thoughts, emotions, and sensations, which can lead to symptoms of depression and anxiety.

Self-kindness refers to being loving, gentle, and accepting toward ourselves when we face personal limitations. It involves having internal dialogues that are encouraging and comforting instead of self-critical. It also entails active self-soothing in times of distress. This contrasts with self-judgment, which involves self-criticism when we are assessing our personal experiences. Unlike self-kindness, self-judgment is likely to result in feelings of shame, leaving us feeling unworthy or defective, which can lead to increased feelings of isolation and loneliness.

Common humanity refers to recognizing that everybody experiences discomfort, pain, and suffering at some point. It reminds us that we are not the only one going through hard things. In fact, failure and perceived flaws are part of our existence, and we all struggle with feelings like shame and insecurity. When we can acknowledge the vulnerability of being human, we tend to feel less isolated and alone because we understand that what makes us feel different is what we actually have in common, which is the opposite of feeling isolated.

What self-compassion is not

There are many misconceptions about self-compassion that might make you doubt its benefits. For example, you might associate self-compassion with self-pity, thinking that by acknowledging your discomfort or pain and responding with care and understanding, you will become self-absorbed or self-indulgent. If you feel that way, I have really good news for you: there is strong evidence showing us the contrary. It turns out, the more self-compassionate we are, the less likely we are to get absorbed in our distress and the more likely we are to keep a broader perspective on situations. So self-compassion is not having a "poor me" attitude at all but rather having an outlook that takes into consideration that suffering is part of being alive— something we all go through. Similarly, self-compassion does not lead to self-indulging behaviors, because it is not a momentary "fix" but rather a long-term capacity to care for ourselves. More precisely, the higher our levels of self-compassion, the more likely we are to have healthier eating patterns, exercise more, and be more intentional when it comes to our physical and emotional wellbeing—all habits with long-term benefits.

Another common misconception is that self-compassion is selfish. Actually, it is quite the opposite because it gives us more to give. Taking care of ourselves doesn't take away from others; it just helps us recharge, stay grounded, and remain emotionally available, rather than retreating and isolating. So the more self-compassionate we are, the more capacity we have to show up for others without becoming overwhelmed or burning out. When we can tolerate discomfort and respond to it with kindness and support, which is the essence of self-compassion, we are less likely to shy away from having authentic connections with others, even in situations of conflict or disagreement. Why? Because when we have the capacity to love and care for our own self just as much as we love and care for others, we are not afraid to take other perspectives into consideration and compromise in situations of conflict, which is the opposite of being selfish.

Another popular misconception is that self-compassion is just an excuse to avoid responsibility for making mistakes, like giving ourselves a free pass or letting us off the hook. It turns out, that's not what happens. Self-compassion isn't about ignoring or excusing our mistakes; it is about creating space for both accountability *and* understanding. Self-compassionate people learn from their mistakes without tearing themselves down, because they know that growth doesn't come from shame but from reflection, responsibility, and a willingness to try again. So they are the ones more likely to take responsibility for their actions, admit their mistakes, and apologize for hurting someone.

Another myth is that self-compassion undermines motivation. In other words, if we are too kind to ourselves, we will lower our standards, get lazy, and stop trying. For this reason, many use self-criticism instead of self-compassion as a motivator. But motivation doesn't thrive on shame; it thrives on support. When we treat ourselves with kindness, we create a safer space to take risks and keep going even after we make mistakes or experience failure. In essence, self-compassion fuels sustainable motivation rooted in care and support, not in fear of harsh self-criticism and blame. We can be both self-compassionate *and* ambitious because self-compassion supports our motivation.

As you can see, self-compassion doesn't make us weak; it is a steady inner source of strength that we can tap into, especially when everything else feels uncertain. It is a quiet kind of strength, always available to us, even in our most vulnerable moments. It doesn't demand perfection, but it offers support, strengthening our ability to remain centered when faced with adversity.

Being kind to yourself changes everything

Many people believe that being hard on ourselves is the only way to move forward or succeed. We fear that if we are not constantly pushing, criticizing, or comparing ourselves with others, we will lose motivation and fall behind. So in this context, the idea of acknowledging our limitations and being kind, supportive, and caring toward ourselves might feel completely terrifying. The good news is that both research and lived experiences tell us that being kind to ourselves, especially in challenging times, is one of the most powerful things we can do for our overall wellbeing. Let's explore why that is…

First and foremost, self-compassion is good for your mind. Studies have shown repeatedly that self-compassion leads to significant mental health benefits. For instance, people who are self-compassionate tend to feel better about their lives than those who are less self-compassionate. They tend to live in greater alignment with their values, experience more pleasant emotions and increased vitality, feel more competent, and have a higher sense of self-worth and self-esteem. Additionally, they experience fewer symptoms of depression, anxiety, or disordered eating—all struggles rooted in shame, which feeds on criticism. Self-compassion can have a powerful soothing effect, even in more extreme cases, like panic attacks or post-traumatic stress, because it gives us space to feel, process, and move through the experience instead of getting stuck in fear or self-blame.

Self-compassion doesn't just help our mind; it also helps our body. For example, it balances the nervous system, helping us handle stress more efficiently. In one study where people were exposed to social stress, those with higher self-compassion recovered faster physically; their heart rate variability stayed more stable, which is a sign of better stress regulation. Even in the case of chronic illnesses like diabetes, those who practiced self-compassion had lower blood sugar levels and felt less overwhelmed by managing their condition. As we age, self-compassion becomes even more important because it acts as a protector against the negative effects that come with physical decline and age-related health issues.

Self-compassion not only affects our inner world; it also makes our relationships better. When we are more self-compassionate, we are actually more compassionate toward others. Why? Because when we are not drained by our own self-criticism, we have more emotional energy to support those around us without becoming overwhelmed. That is to say, self-compassion makes us more emotionally available and present for others. Studies show that people with higher levels of self-compassion tend to show up more authentically with others—they are more open, express their wants and desires more clearly, and are better at balancing their own needs with the needs of others. For example, in romantic relationships, they not only recognize their partner's needs are equally as important as their own but also trust that their significant other will care about what matters to them. Even during conflict, they feel more authentic as they experience less emotional turmoil, approaching problems constructively and being willing to compromise. This is in contrast to those less self-compassionate, who often approach problems with doubt, avoidance, or self-blame, lacking confidence and being less willing to take responsibility in solving the problem.

When looking at the benefits of self-compassion, the big takeaway is that self-compassion isn't just a nice idea but a powerful tool for real, long-lasting wellbeing. When we practice self-compassion, we support our mental health by increasing positive mood and reducing anxiety and depression; we care for our physical health by modulating our body's stress response and even improving outcomes in chronic illness; and we nourish our relationships by showing up more authentically and offering others the same kindness we give ourselves. But the story doesn't end here—self-compassion becomes a superpower when it meets shame.

Self-compassion: The antidote to shame

Shame has the power to convince us that failure and mistakes are not just something that we experience, but something *we are*. During those tender moments, we tend to isolate and hide the parts of ourselves we are most afraid of being seen. So we protect ourselves by shutting down or pretending we are fine. The thing is, shame feeds on silence—it grows when we keep it quiet, keeping us stuck in the belief that we need to hide who we really are because who we are is not enough.

Unlike shame, self-compassion gently invites us to show up just as we are, without needing to hide or punish ourselves. When self-compassion meets shame, it doesn't just soften its grip; it actively rewrites the story it tries to tell us. Exactly what shame takes away from us— connection, acceptance, and worthiness—self-compassion is offering in abundance. When shame tells us, "You're not good enough," self-compassion says, "Yes, you made a mistake, but that doesn't make you less worthy." When shame utters, "You're unlovable," self-compassion whispers, "You feel unlovable, and you are hurting. This is deeply human, and you deserve love and kindness just as you are." When shame shouts, "You are broken," self-compassion responds gently, "You are struggling and feeling broken, and like anyone in pain you need care and support, not criticism."

While shame tells us there is something wrong with us at our core, that we are unlovable and not enough, self-compassion reminds us we are human and worthy of love and support, especially in moments when we feel the most broken. So instead of isolating and spiraling into self-blame, self-compassion helps us see that struggles are part of being human, inviting us to respond to our pain the same way we would to someone we love. Put another way, self-compassion interrupts the cycle of self-blaming by holding space for the simple fact that suffering is part of life, not a sign that something is wrong with us. Self-compassion helps quiet the inner critic and turns up the gentle voice that soothes the emotional distress caused by shame.

Self-compassion is not a fix; it is a way of being *with* ourselves exactly as we are, standing by ourselves not only when we shine but also when we stumble. It is replacing harsh judgment with empathy and pressure with patience. Self-compassion is a practice we need to return to again and again because life will keep offering us moments that will make us doubt our value and question our worth. And when that happens, we need self-compassion to remind us of what shame makes us forget: that we are already enough, just as we are.

PART 2

The Practice

THE ART IN SELF-REGULATION PRACTICE

The first part of this book focused on foundational information about what influences our physical, mental, and emotional states. Specifically, what regulates or dysregulates us. You now understand the power of our brain in shaping our immediate future, the influence of our early caregiving environment on how we see the world, the benefits of attachment security, how shame can bring us suffering, and why self-compassion can be one of the biggest gifts we can offer ourselves. Although this foundational information is essential for the process of self-regulation, it is not sufficient. What will ultimately bring you inner stability is the *practice* of self-regulation. For that reason, this second part of the book is focused on the ART of self-regulation, the process that includes the practice of **anchoring, reflecting,** and **transforming**.

Anchoring provides us with the experience of being grounded in the present moment—the only moment we have any influence over. The past has already happened, and we can't foresee the future, but we can be intentional in the present moment. Even when external circumstances are beyond our control, we can still use the present moment to modulate our body's reactions, thoughts, and emotions. The practice of anchoring helps us avoid getting caught up in what has happened in the past or what might happen in the future, strengthening our ability to remain anchored in the present and navigate life more effectively.

The process of **reflecting** creates space where we can become aware of and acknowledge our inner experiences instead of ignoring or dismissing them. Through the process of reflection, we give ourselves permission to feel the sensations in our body, observe the quality of our thoughts, and witness our emotions without judgment. It provides the opportunity to become attuned to our inner world, increasing our ability to notice early signs of distress before they escalate. Oftentimes, the body sends us signals of dysregulation before we are even aware of our thoughts and emotions. A tense body or fatigue might indicate that our body budget is running on a deficit. A racing heart, shallow breathing, or tightness in the stomach might indicate that we are stressed, anxious, or afraid. Similarly, a headache might indicate overthinking.

Besides our body's signals, we might notice that we focus on the worst-case scenarios or have self-defeating internal dialogues. We might also identify that we are experiencing difficult emotions or notice feeling numb and disconnected. Whatever awareness arises from the process of reflection, it provides the opportunity to intervene and restore internal balance.

The process of **transforming** begins when we create new and positive experiences that the brain can use to create new predictions. By intentionally creating new experiences of balance, joy, gratitude, awe, ease, and love, we can thoughtfully shape the life we desire and become the person we want to be. The intention behind this process goes beyond creating a nourishing present and future. This process can transform our past by creating a better one through how we choose to live in each moment. So when we look back on our life, we can proudly say that we created a work of art.

The ART of self-regulation symbolizes the idea that our life is a work of art. Like any creation, we need to approach it with the understanding that it is not a linear, rigid, or mechanical process but rather nuanced, sophisticated, and surprising at times. So it requires a thoughtful approach and the skillfulness to meet our needs in ways that serve us best.

The 21-day practice

For the next 21 days, I will introduce you to the ART of self-regulation. For the first seven days, you will use **anchoring** as a tool to ground yourself in the present moment and to create spaces you can safely retreat to in times of distress. You will use the five senses, the breath, the power of self-compassion, the flow of writing, the magic of imagination, the energy of movement, and whatever else feels good to you. Then, for another seven days, you will dive into **reflecting** on your inner world. First, you will identify your attachment style to better understand why you see and interact with yourself and others the way you do, and why you might find yourself in continuous cycles of turmoil. Knowing your attachment style is important because it empowers you to take intentional steps toward earned security.

Gaining the awareness you may have an insecure attachment might come with difficult emotions, such as worry, sadness, grief, or anger. Whatever emotions might arise, there will be space for them to be acknowledged, felt, and held with kindness and care. There will also be space to listen to the gentle voice within that carries wisdom and can guide you in difficult times—an inner source of comfort when needed. You will also acknowledge the harsh and judgmental internal voice that can sometimes hurt and shame us in ways that are difficult to bear. You will create space to identify cues of dysregulation but also acknowledge how you feel when you are calm. Finally, you will develop a practice of noticing the good things that are already happening in your life.

The seven days of reflection will be followed by seven days of **transforming** your experiences. The process of transformation will include the practice of regulating your body, thoughts, emotions, and attention. During this time, you will also be intentional in choosing what feels good, observing your experiences, and purposely slowing down to rest, rejuvenate, and savor all the good things that you already have in your life.

On each day of this 21-day practice of self-regulation, I will guide your steps by providing you with a daily topic of focus, the rationale for choosing that topic, and an experiential activity that will ultimately lead you to the embodied experience of the ART of self-regulation. Some of the experiential activities require you to have a notebook, a pen, and a quiet place where you won't be interrupted. Each daily practice will take between 20 and 60 minutes, but you can tailor the time based on your own unique needs.

Although not necessary, it might be helpful to set aside a specific time each day to practice so you can find a rhythm that works for you over the next 21 days. Setting aside a specific time each day to practice helps create consistency, which is key for building new habits. When practice becomes part of your daily routine, it is less likely to get pushed aside. It also helps your brain anticipate the practice, making it feel more natural and grounded over time. Finding a rhythm that works for you during the next 21 days can also make this journey feel more intentional rather than something you are squeezing in last minute or forgetting altogether.

With that being said, there is no right or wrong way of practicing the ART of self-regulation—your way will be the best way for you.

DAYS 1–7

Anchoring: The Power of Grounding

"We need to be able to be fully present in our body and brain together to make the best choices and to help our emotional regulation."

Dr. Tara Swart

For the next seven days, you will experience the power of grounding in the present moment through various forms of **anchoring**.

Day 1: You will practice using your five senses to connect to the external world.

Day 2: You will practice various types of breathing that can help you intentionally adjust your level of alertness in real time.

Day 3: You will experience the power of self-compassion to transform a moment of suffering into one of supportive care.

Day 4: You will practice being present in the moment and connecting with your inner experience through writing.

Day 5: You will create a space that serves as a sanctuary, available to be used whenever needed.

Day 6: You will practice intentional movement that connects you to your body.

Day 7: You will practice anchoring yourself in what feels good, intentionally seeking out those experiences and embracing them as often as you need or want to.

All these practices of anchoring are intended to offer support when things become difficult or out of control. The more we cultivate our ability to anchor ourselves in the present moment and connect with our experiences, the more we expand our capacity to maintain a sense of steadiness, even during challenging times.

DAY 1

Anchor in your senses: Back to basics

"We are born as feeling creatures. We feel before we think."

Dr. Gabor Maté

Have you ever had an argument with someone and continued to argue with that person in your mind days after the quarrel ended, playing out hypothetical scenarios, going back and forth between what you said or what you could've said instead? If you did, don't worry— you are in good company. We all find ourselves in those situations at times, trapped in loops of thoughts and emotions, running through virtual realities in our mind that have never happened and most likely never will. Ruminating on the past or worrying about the future disconnects us from the present moment, making us feel as if we are out of control or removed from reality.

The good news is we can always interrupt the loops of thoughts and emotions by giving the brain something immediate and neutral to focus on, such as the physical environment around us. We can use our five senses— sight, hearing, smell, taste, and touch—to really notice our surroundings, one sense at a time. This intentional focus on what we see, hear, smell, taste, or touch forces the mind to stop ruminating on the past or worrying about the future, centering us in the *here and now*. Simply put, focusing on our senses is an instant way to reconnect with the present moment.

The beauty of anchoring in the five senses is that we can do it *anywhere*. For instance, we can be at home, eating a snack, focusing on its taste, smell, and texture. Or we can be in the park, listening to the sound of birds, feeling the warmth of the sun on our skin or the crisp, cold air on our face. We can even be in the office, noticing shapes, colors, and textures, focusing on our body touching the chair or our clothes touching our skin. We can feel the soles of our feet while standing, sitting, taking a walk, or running. Wherever we are and whatever we are doing, our senses will always be there to help us shift our attention from our internal experience to the external world when needed.

Experiential activity

Today's practice is focused on the experience of anchoring in the present moment through the five senses: sight, hearing, smell, taste, and touch. This practice has several prompts I invite you to follow. There is no right or wrong way to go through this practice, so allow yourself to engage in it freely and without any restrictions. Before you start, take a few deep breaths, letting go of any unnecessary tension in your body.

Now, ask yourself the following questions:

What do I see?

- Take a few moments to look around and really notice your environment—perhaps you can see a table, a book, a pen, a cup, a plant, or the light coming through the window. Take your time to notice any physical object that you can see at the time. If you prefer, you can focus on one single object and observe the details of that object such as its shape, size, color, or texture.

- When you are ready, take a deep breath in, let it all out, and then gently move your attention to the sense of hearing.

What do I hear?

- Now I invite you to allow the sense of hearing to enter your awareness, paying attention to any of the sounds around you, whether they are subtle or loud. You might hear the hum of the refrigerator, air conditioner, or heater, or perhaps the traffic in the distance, the birds chirping outside, the sound of your own breathing, or some other random background noise. Whatever sounds you can hear, really tune in to each sound, one at a time, without any judgment, just listening. If it helps, you can close your eyes during this part of the exercise.

- When you are ready, take a deep breath in, let it all out, and then gently move your attention to the sense of smell.

What do I smell?

- This time, I invite you to take a few moments to allow the sense of smell to enter your awareness, really paying attention to any scents in the air around you. You might notice the quality of the air in the room—fresh or stuffy, the scent of flowers, or the delicious aroma of food cooking. If you like, you can light a candle or use your favorite hand lotion or essential oils to enhance your experience of anchoring in your sense of smell. If it helps, you can choose to close your eyes and allow only the sense of smell to enter your experience.

- When you are ready, take a deep breath in, let it all out, and then gently move your attention to the sense of taste.

What do I taste?

- Now I invite you to take a few moments to allow the sense of taste to enter your awareness, taking time to notice any tastes in your mouth. You might notice a lingering taste from the most recent meal or drink you had. If that is not the case, simply notice the lack of flavor or perhaps the moisture or the dryness in your mouth. If you wish, you can chew a piece of gum, take a bite of your favorite snack, or sip on a beverage while paying close attention to the sensation of taste. If closing your eyes during the process enhances your experience, please do so.

- When you are ready, take a deep breath in, let it all out, and then gently move your attention to the sense of touch.

What do I touch?

- Now I invite you to take a few moments to let the sense of touch enter your awareness, paying close attention to any sensations you can feel—the soles of your feet touching the ground, your clothes touching your body, or skin touching on skin. You can also notice the places where your body is touching the surface that supports you, perhaps a chair, a bed, or the ground. You can touch the objects around you with your hands, feeling the textures of the objects and the pressure of your hands on those objects. Or you can simply notice the temperature of the air on your skin.

- When you are ready, take the deepest breath you have taken all day and let this practice settle in. You can come back to this practice whenever you need to slow down and reconnect with the present.

DAY 2

Anchor in your breathing: Patterns of breathing

"How we breathe matters."

James Nestor

The breath is known to be one of the most powerful tools we can use to anchor ourselves in the present moment. Just like with the five senses, we can use our breath as something immediate and neutral to focus on to interrupt loops of unpleasant thoughts and emotions. This intentional focus on our breath stops the mind from ruminating and instantly connects us back to the present moment.

We can also use our breath to adjust our level of alertness in real time by using specific patterns of breathing. We can do that because we have the kind of biology that allows us to modify our heart rate through the diaphragm. For example, if we want to feel more energized, our inhales need to be longer than our exhales, and if we want to feel more relaxed, then our exhales need to be longer than our inhales. This is how it works: when we inhale, our lungs expand and our diaphragm is pushed down, which provides our heart with more space to expand so the blood flows through the heart more slowly, which sends our brain the signal that it needs to speed up the heartbeat. When we exhale, our diaphragm moves up, creating a smaller space for our heart and, as a result, the blood flows more quickly through the heart, signaling to our brain that the heart needs to slow down. This communication between the body and the brain can speed the heart rate up or down based on the breathing pattern. Knowing this, we can be intentional about the type of breathing pattern we use in different situations. For instance, if we feel nervous, angry, or worried, we can use patterns of breathing that relax the body, whereas if we feel lethargic or bored, we can use patterns of breathing that increase our energy levels.

The beauty of using the breath to anchor ourselves in the present moment is that we can do it anywhere. We can be at home, at work, out and about with our friends, on a plane, or in a car. Wherever we are, our breath is with us, ready to be used in ways that serve us best.

Experiential activity

In today's practice, you will experience four patterns of breathing that you can always use based on your immediate needs. Although intentional breathing patterns are very useful tools to maintain or modify the state we are in, there are people who might find anchoring in the breath challenging. If you find yourself in that situation, don't worry. There are many other anchoring strategies that you will learn this week and could use when needed.

Physiological sigh

For this pattern of breathing, I invite you to take a deep breath in, immediately followed by another one and then exhale completely. Repeat this pattern of breathing a few times or as much as needed, since it might take about 20–30 seconds for your heart rate to go back to its baseline. The role of the physiological sigh is to expel a higher quantity of carbon dioxide from the body for immediate relaxation. The physiological sigh is known to be the fastest way to relax the nervous system, so please take your time to practice it throughout the day.

Relaxing breathing

Now you will experience a pattern of breathing that you can use when you want to relax your body, such as when you feel frustrated, furious, provoked, nervous, or worried. For this pattern of breathing, I invite you to inhale for four seconds and exhale for eight seconds. Take your time and repeat this way of breathing a few times. Sometimes, in really difficult situations, you might need to repeat this breathing pattern for longer to help your body regain a sense of calmness.

Energizing breathing

Now I invite you to experience a pattern of breathing you can use when you experience low levels of energy, such as when you are feeling tired, lethargic, apathetic, or sleepy, but still need to focus or get work done. For this pattern of breathing, I invite you to inhale vigorously for four seconds and exhale for two seconds. You might notice some dizziness when breathing this way, which is common, especially if you're new to it. So make sure to listen to your body and take breaks as needed. Like with any other pattern of breathing, repeat the process a few times or for as long as needed to feel energized.

Coherent breathing

Finally, I invite you to experience the type of breathing you can use when you are in a state of balance and you want to maintain it. All you need to do is keep your inhales and exhales equally long—for example, inhale for five seconds and exhale for five seconds. Just like with all the other breathing types, repeat the process a few times or for as long as you need to.

DAY 3

Anchor in yourself: Gestures of self-compassion

*"A moment of self-compassion can change your entire day.
A string of such moments can change the course of your life."*

Dr. Christopher Germer

Self-compassion is one of the biggest gifts we can offer ourselves in times of distress. Just like we bring ease to a friend who is struggling by holding them in a warm embrace or providing words of encouragement, we can bring ease and comfort to our own self. Simple gestures of support can help us reconnect with our own self in a supportive and nurturing way, providing us with a sense of safety and warmth.

Offering ourselves compassion can make us feel vulnerable, which we might interpret as weakness; however, vulnerability is not weakness. If anything, it is a strength because it allows us to acknowledge and be open to our own struggle, creating the opportunity for authenticity, healing, and growth. By offering gestures of self-compassion, we allow ourselves to have empathy for our experiences and be more realistic in acknowledging that we, just like any other human being, have limitations and imperfections, and that doesn't make us less worthy of love and care. Self-compassion encourages us to embrace our imperfections, which might feel unsettling for those who seek perfection. If that happens, remember that perfection doesn't exist. Only by allowing ourselves to embrace our limitations can we progress in difficult times.

The idea of offering kindness to yourself when things go wrong might feel uncomfortable at first, especially if your tendency is to avoid or suppress difficult emotions. Self-compassion can be anxiety-provoking for those with a history of neglect and abuse who were not allowed to comfort themselves, and for whom soothing was not accessible. If during the practice of self-compassion you experience discomfort, please don't get discouraged. Be patient with yourself because, just like with any new practice, the practice of being kind to yourself takes time. As you continue to practice, self-compassion will slowly become a new way of being.

Today, I invite you to give yourself permission to experience the initial discomfort that might arise and trust that the gestures of self-compassion won't make you weak or self-indulgent. Actually, the opposite is true— these gestures will add to your resilience and emotional strength and, as a result, give you a more sustainable sense of stability. In difficult times, these gestures can be a reminder that you, just like everyone else, are worthy of love, understanding, and care, and wherever you are or wherever you go, you always have your own self to rely on.

Experiential activity

In today's practice, you will experience anchoring in gestures of self-compassion. Each of the following gestures of self-compassion provides a physical and emotional expression of care, a way of responding to pain and suffering with love and support rather than judgment and criticism. This practice has several prompts and there is no right or wrong way to go through it, so allow yourself to engage in it freely and without any restrictions. Before you start, I invite you to take a few deep breaths, letting go of any unnecessary tension in your body.

Gentle touch

The gentle touch can be both soothing and supportive, and it is always available for us to use for comfort and support. Gently placing your hands over any part of your body is one of the most powerful physical gestures of self-compassion. The act of softly touching your body can create a sense of comfort and connection similar to an embrace received from a loved one.

First, I invite you to simply rest one or both hands over your heart. Take a minute or so to feel the warmth and gentle pressure of your touch, reminding yourself that you are worthy of kindness and care, just like any other human being. Then, place your hands over your belly, repeating the same gentle pressure, feeling the warmth of your hands and the support of your touch. After a minute or so, place your hands over your cheeks, holding your face as you would hold the face of a loved one, feeling the care and love that comes with it. Then you can use the same gentle touch over your arms, your shoulders, or any other place on your body that might need comforting. As you are going through each gentle touch, take your time to feel which of them provides you with the most comfort and support. During this practice, you can close your eyes partially or fully, allowing yourself to fully connect with your inner experience.

Self-hug

Hugging ourselves can help us feel nurtured and safe, just as we would feel in the embrace of a loved one. Through self-hugging we communicate that we are there for our own self, offering care and support when feeling vulnerable. Now I invite you to wrap your arms around yourself, holding yourself in a gentle hug. You might choose to close your eyes partially or fully and sway slowly back and forth to add to the experience of comfort. Please take your time to rest in this warm embrace and connect with your inner experience.

Gentle massage

A gentle massage of the parts of your body that feel tense can alleviate discomfort and have a soothing effect on your body. So I invite you to gently massage your head, temples, neck, shoulders, arms, hands, or feet, focusing on the light pressure of your hands and the care you are providing to yourself. As you are massaging these areas of your body, you can close your eyes and start to breathe slowly and deeply. Allow yourself some time to fully experience the effects of this gentle massage on your body.

Kind words of support

Using our inner voice to speak to ourselves in a gentle, understanding, and supportive tone can have a significant positive impact on how we feel about ourselves. In moments of struggle, we can use kind words of support such as:

- *"I'm allowed to have bad days, just like everyone else."*
- *"I am worthy of love and care, even when I make mistakes."*
- *"It is okay not to have all the answers right now."*
- *"This moment doesn't define me."*
- *"I am enough just as I am."*

- *"I don't have to be perfect to be worthy of love and care."*

- *"I have been through a lot and it is okay to feel tired."*

- *"It is okay to be kind to myself."*

- *"I'm only human. It is okay to make mistakes."*

- *"Everyone has moments of struggle. I'm not alone in this."*

- *"Pain and discomfort are part of the human experience."*

I invite you to use these words if they resonate with you, or create your own soothing phrases. Allow yourself time to find the words that have the most comforting effect on you, then close your eyes and whisper them to yourself.

DAY 4

Anchor in writing: Journaling

*"Keeping a journal will absolutely change your life
in ways you've never imagined."*

Oprah Winfrey

Journaling is a profound practice that anchors us in the present moment, fostering a deeper connection to our inner experience. Writing our thoughts on paper helps us slow down, allowing space for thoughts to form, organize, and be processed in a coherent way. Think of the page as a space that can hold our emotions, thoughts, intentions, worries, celebrations, or life-changing events. Over time, the page can become the place where we show up just the way we are and trust that it will always be there, without judgment.

The good news is you don't have to be a writer to journal. You don't even have to like writing; you just need to know how to write. Journaling is not about writing eloquent phrases, well thought-out ideas, or grammatically correct sentences with appropriate punctuation. It is about allowing your thoughts to be written on the page just as they are, without judgment or expectations.

Through journaling we develop awareness of our inner experiences. We observe whether we overidentify with or ruminate on thoughts and emotions, creating unnecessary suffering, or whether we tend to dismiss them to avoid facing discomfort and pain. Journaling also helps us observe the stability versus the transiency of our thoughts and emotions. The stability of our thoughts reveals the beliefs we hold, and the notebook page can be the place where we can reflect on these beliefs, question them if necessary, and observe if there are any discrepancies between our beliefs and our actions.

On the other hand, the transiency of our thoughts can help us realize that thoughts and ideas are continuously influenced and changed by our internal states such as sensations in the body, emotions, or memories. Our thoughts are also influenced by external factors such as interactions with others, the news we receive from people close to us or the world at large, the quality of our environment, or unexpected events. In short, journaling is a powerful tool for self-reflection that we can all use daily, weekly, or monthly. There are no rules about how often or for how long you need to write, or what to write about. If you've never journaled before, don't worry—below you will find some guidance on where to start.

First, I invite you to find a notebook. It can be small or large, a fancy one designed for journaling or a simple ruled notebook that you can find at any store. Over the years, I have written in all types of notebooks, and I've learned that the notebook itself doesn't really matter in the journaling process. It is the practice of journaling that makes the difference.

Once you have your notebook, the next step is to find a pen to write with. Just like with the notebook, there are no requirements regarding what type of pen to use. It can be a ballpoint, gel, or fountain pen with black, blue, red, or purple ink—whatever feels good to you. The only thing you want to be mindful of is choosing a pen that works well so the flow of writing will not be interrupted by it.

Once you've found a notebook and a pen, I invite you to find a quiet place where you can write. If a quiet place is not really an option for you, at least find somewhere you won't be interrupted by others. Over the years, I have learned that, based on what I am going through, I sometimes need a quiet place to write, while other times I can be in the middle of a busy airport and write completely undisturbed.

Experiential activity

Landing on the page is the first step in the process of journaling and sometimes the hardest part. So, if you find yourself staring at a blank page, not knowing where to start, don't worry—I will guide you as we go.

First, write the date and the time in the top-right corner of the page. Now, you might wonder what your first sentence should be about, so I invite you to take a few moments to observe your thoughts and then write them down. For example, *This is weird. I have no idea what I am doing… What thoughts? There are no thoughts to observe… I don't think this will work for me. I really don't know what to write about… What should I write about? What thoughts do I have?*

Hmmm… I don't really like this. This is stupid. I'm not good at writing… Let's see… What are my thoughts?… So this is what I should write down? What are my thoughts? Okay, I can do that… Maybe this will work. I have heard people say that journaling is good for you. Even Oprah is saying it, so it must be true.

All the examples above are a perfect place to start. Observe one thought after another and write them down without judgment. Like the start of anything, it takes a bit of time and practice to find a rhythm. At first, your thoughts will be about the newness of the practice, and that's what you will notice, just as in the examples provided above. Over time, the page will become a familiar and comfortable place where you can rest in the present moment. Just like in all the other practices you have learned so far, the key is to come back to the present moment, the only moment we have influence over.

Please start the process of journaling as small as you want to—one sentence, two sentences, half a page, a whole page, or just write for as long as it feels good. Set a realistic goal for yourself and meet that goal even if all you write is… *I have no idea what to write about, but I set a goal for myself to write ten sentences and here I am trying to meet that goal. This is stupid but Nicoleta said it is going to work, so I am doing it. There are six more sentences I need to write to meet my goal. I don't have any more thoughts, I don't feel anything. I don't want to think about my day. I don't really like my day. It is hard to write. I don't like hard things… I wrote nine sentences. I did it!*

The key is not how long you write for, but how often you come back to the page. Trust that the initial awkwardness will dissipate with time and comfort will take its place.

DAY 5

Anchor in safety: A special place

"Everything you can imagine is real."

Pablo Picasso

Today's focus is on creating a place that feels good to you. A place in which you might feel protected, calm, content, joyful, safe, or happy. This place will serve as a space in which you can retreat to maintain or regain balance when faced with challenges. In this place, you can find safety when you feel vulnerable, calm when you feel overwhelmed, protected when you feel afraid, unconditional love when you feel embarrassed, cared for when you feel rejected, or hopeful when you feel despair. This place can be a physical place that you are already familiar with or have access to. For example, it might be a house or a room in a house. It can be a place in nature, a garden, a park, a forest, a beach, a mountain, a meadow, or a wildflower field. It can be a spiritual site, such as a church, a temple, a mosque, or a monastery. It can also be a therapist's room, a support group, a library, a quiet meditation room, or any other place that feels safe to you.

This place can also be an imaginary one you create in your own mind. Think of it as your own sanctuary that you can travel to within seconds from wherever you are, just by closing your eyes. You can create this place based on your own needs and include in it whatever makes you feel good, without any restrictions. For example, you can use elements of nature such as a garden in the spring, blooming flowers filling the air with nectar-like sweetness, a bed of soft grass in a meadow on a summer day, soothing sounds of rustling leaves in the forest, chirping birds, the rhythmic flow of the ocean waves, a mountaintop with a breathtaking panoramic landscape, or the gaze of bright stars on a summer night. There is no limit to what you can add to the place you are creating for yourself.

This place can also include people who make you feel good. You might already have a special person in your life who you trust and feel safe with—perhaps a family member, a friend, a mentor, a therapist, a spiritual being, or whoever supports and genuinely cares about you. If you do have such a special person in your life, you already know that sometimes being in the presence of this person is all you need to feel a sense of balance. If you don't have someone like this in your life, imagine a person that has all the qualities you need them to have, perhaps someone who is understanding, kind, loving, caring, and wise, who makes you feel calm, joyful, peaceful, safe, happy, playful, comfortable, or whichever emotion you enjoy the most. Whenever you experience difficult feelings, you can use this place as an anchor to keep you from floating away in deep states of distress.

Experiential activity

For today's practice, I invite you to find a quiet place, and if that is not an option for you, at least find somewhere you can spend some uninterrupted time. You can use your journal; however, it is not necessary unless you want to use writing as part of the process. Before you start, I invite you to take a few deep breaths, letting go of any unnecessary tension in your body.

Now, please take time to allow yourself to find that very special place that can bring you pleasant emotions, such as calm, joy, peace, safety, happiness, playfulness, comfort, or whichever emotion you enjoy the most. Imagine this place as being your own sanctuary.

While going through the process of creating your special place, answer the questions below and imagine all the elements that bring this place to life.

- What colors do you see?
- What sounds can you hear?
- What aromas can you sense?
- What tastes can you experience?
- What's the temperature of this place?
- What textures can you feel?
- Is there anyone else there, or is this place only for you?
- What conversations do you have?
- Who do you have these dialogues with?
- Are there any rules in this place, or perhaps there are no rules at all?

Remember, this place is your sanctuary, and you can create it as you want it to be. Once created, this will always be your sacred space that you can retreat to just by closing your eyes.

Day 6

Anchor in movement: Intentional movement

"Walk as if you are kissing the Earth with your feet."

Thich Nhat Hanh

Moving with intention is a powerful way to anchor ourselves in the present moment, especially during challenging times. Usually, in times of distress, the mind tends to race and the body tenses up. When that happens, we can use movement to reconnect with our body and also help our mind take a break from endless loops of rumination. Movement helps us anchor in the present moment by connecting us with the sensations in our body.

Intentional movement does not require sophisticated activity or advanced exercise. The movement can be gentle, slow, and easy. It is the mindfulness and care that is more important rather than the intensity of the physical activity. The goal of this type of movement is to focus on the here and now, switching from being on "autopilot" to a sense of presence. When we move with intention, we start to become more aware of the sensations in our body rather than the thoughts that are causing stress, helping us to let go of mental clutter and become more grounded in the present.

Experiential activity

Today, I invite you to choose a few movements that feel good to you and bring your body ease and comfort. You might not feel like moving today, but I invite you to do it anyway so you can feel the benefits of intentional movement in your body. The whole purpose of today's practice is to move with intention, regardless of the type of movement you choose. Below are a few examples of gentle movements you can pick from to use today. If there are other types of movement that you already enjoy, use those instead.

Today's practice has several guiding prompts. There is no right or wrong way to go through this practice, so allow yourself to engage in it freely and without any restrictions. Before you start, I invite you to take a few deep breaths, letting go of any unnecessary tension in your body.

Walking

Go outside and take a walk. Do it alone and without distractions, meaning with no music or talking on the phone. As you are walking, slow down and pay attention to each step you are taking. As your feet connect with the ground, notice the shift in weight as you put each foot in front of the other, the pressure on the soles of your feet, and the slow rhythm of your movement. Take each step as an opportunity to stay connected to the present moment. Your walk can be as long or as short as you want it to be.

Swaying or dancing

Not a dancer? No worries. This type of swaying, or dancing, is for everyone. Just put your favorite music on and start swaying your body, letting go of any judgment or expectation. Let the music move your body, from the soles of your feet all the way to the top of your head, allowing your arms to flow and your hips to follow the rhythm of the music. Move freely and simply express yourself through movement, allowing your body to flow with the beat. Let this gentle movement connect you with your body. Trust your body's wisdom, and dance with joy, freedom, and presence in every moment. Dance like nobody's watching.

Gentle stretching

Gentle stretching can be done standing, sitting, or lying down, depending on what type of stretch you choose to do. At any time during this gentle movement, you can close your eyes partially or fully. Before starting to stretch, take a few deep, slow breaths, letting your body relax with each breath. You can start by moving your head gently toward each shoulder, feeling a light stretch in your neck. Hold the stretch for a few seconds while breathing deeply. With each stretch, feel the gentle release of tension in your neck. If it feels good, you can begin rolling your head slowly by gently dropping your chin toward your chest and then toward your right shoulder, and all the way back to your chest, feeling the gentle stretch in the back of your neck. You can continue by moving your head in a full circle. After a few rotations, reverse the direction, moving slowly and with intention, allowing each roll to release any tension in your neck and shoulders.

Next, you can roll your shoulders backward in a circular motion, starting with small circles followed by larger ones. After a few seconds, reverse the direction and roll your shoulders forwards for another few seconds. Breathe deeply and let go of any unnecessary tension in your shoulders.

Now, place your feet on the ground while sitting or standing. Extend your arms above your head and gently bring your hands together and interlace your fingers, turning your palms to face up. Start to lean gently to one side and then the other, feeling the stretch along the sides of your body. Breathe deeply and hold each stretch for a few seconds.

Now, place your feet on the ground while sitting or standing, and allow your body to fold forward, reaching your hands as far as it feels comfortable toward your shins or your toes. You can bend your knees as generously as you want to, feeling the gentle stretch in your lower back and the backs of your legs. Breathe deeply and stay in this forward fold for a few seconds or for as long as it feels good.

Next, move into a tabletop position for a cat-cow stretch, with your hands directly under your shoulders and knees under your hips to create a stable base. As you inhale deeply, start tilting your tailbone toward the ceiling, allowing your belly to drop toward the floor, arching your lower back like a lazy cat that just woke up from a nap. Lift your chest forward and open through the heart, drawing the shoulder blades down your back. Imagine creating a "U" shape in your spine from your tailbone to the crown of your head. Then, as you exhale, tuck your chin toward your chest and start rounding your back upward, feeling the gentle stretch in your back. Imagine creating an arch with your spine from your tailbone to the crown of your head. With each movement, take a deep breath in through your nose, followed by a slow exhale through your mouth, letting go of any unnecessary tension in your body. If it feels good, you can gently rock your hips from side to side as you move through this pose. Flow through this movement at your own pace for as long as it feels good.

Next, sit on the floor with your legs out in front of you, bending your knees as generously as you want. Lean forward and reach for your shins and toes, feeling a gentle stretch across your back. Round your back and relax in this position for as long as it feels good.

Lastly, lie on your back with your hands a few inches away from your body and your legs hip-width apart. Start moving your wrists in a circular motion a few times, then do the same with your ankles. When you are done, allow your body to be still and relax completely. Stay in this final position for as long as it feels good.

DAY 7

Anchor in what feels good

"Every day may not be good... but there's something good in every day."

Alice Morse Earle

Being aware of what makes us feel good can be very powerful because we can then seek those things with intention and anchor in them as often as we want or need to. There are things we experience daily that have a soothing effect on our body; we just need to be aware of them. Think of the warmth of the sun on your skin, the chirping of the birds, the white clouds moving over a clear blue sky, the warm colors of the sunset, the stars on a clear night, the changing colors of the leaves in the fall, the sound of the rain, the scent of blooming plants, the crisp air on an early morning, the snow falling quietly from the sky, or the taste of fresh fruit. All these are elements of nature, parts of our daily lives, that can bring comfort when we pay attention to them.

Besides aspects of nature, there are also things we can do with the intention of bringing a sense of comfort and joy into our life. Think of a warm cup of tea on a cold day, reading a novel or watching a good movie, dancing and laughing, a bubble bath at the end of the day, a delicious meal, a long walk at sunrise or sunset, a quiet morning, a peaceful evening, journaling, hanging out with friends—having no plans other than just being together, spending a whole day in pajamas, sleeping in, taking a nap in the middle of the day, walking barefoot on grass or sand, a massage, a hike, a puzzle, painting, crocheting, a scented candle at night, a piece of dark chocolate, gardening, yoga, good music, playing music, exploring a farmers market, going out for a picnic, falling asleep under a tree, pampering yourself with a facial mask, or mixing your favorite essential oils. The list is endless. Add to this list whatever feels good to you and then try new things that might bring you a sense of wellbeing.

Based on where you are in the world and your own preferences, there are many things that might bring comfort to your body and make you feel connected to yourself and to the present moment. Today's focus is on finding those things that feel good. So I invite you to go through the day noticing what brings you a sense of calm, ease, joy, comfort, thankfulness, inspiration, peace, playfulness, or contentment.

Experiential activity

For today's practice, I invite you to take out your journal and a pen and find a quiet space where you can be comfortable and without distractions. There will be several prompts for reflection, and after each prompt, I invite you to close your eyes for a few moments, allowing yourself to reflect on your answers. There is no right or wrong way to answer the guiding prompts, so allow yourself to engage with the prompt freely and without any restrictions. Before you start, take a few deep breaths, letting go of any unnecessary tension in your body.

Now I invite you to start thinking of things that make you feel good. Identify and write down each element of nature or situation that brings pleasant sensations and comfort to your body, mind, and soul. For instance, you might write:

- *Peaceful mornings*
- *Walking at sunset*
- *The sound of crickets*
- *Chirping birds*
- *Warmth of the sun on my skin*
- *Yoga*
- *Journaling*
- *Massage*
- *Listening to music*

Take your time with this process. There is no need to rush it. As you are going through the list, take time to notice the sensations in your body, your thoughts, and any associated emotions that might arise with each element of nature or situation that feels good to you. If what you are experiencing is pleasant, savor it, and recognize it as a sign to move toward that element or situation. If what you are experiencing is neutral or unpleasant, let go of that thing, and find something else that feels good. Curate your list and only keep what truly makes you feel good because, as you are moving through this journey of self-regulation, you will be using all these things that make you feel good as an anchor during challenging times.

As you are writing your list, consider the following questions:

- What brings me joy?
- What brings me excitement?
- What brings me awe?
- What makes me grateful?
- What makes me happy?
- What makes me feel safe?
- What makes me feel peaceful?
- What makes me feel content?

DAYS 8–14

Reflecting: Your Inner World

"What lies behind us and what lies before us are tiny matters,
compared to what lies within us."

Henry Stanley Haskins

For the next seven days, we will be focusing on **reflecting**: the process of acknowledging and examining our internal experiences with genuine curiosity rather than judgment or criticism.

Day 8: You will learn about your own attachment style.

Day 9: You will create space to accurately identify and label your experiences and differentiate between discomfort and suffering.

Day 10: You will experience the guidance of your inner wisdom.

Day 11: You will create space to reflect on your inner critical voice, its origins, and whether this voice is trying to protect you or it's hurting you.

Day 12: You will experience the process of identifying early signs of dysregulation and reflect on the source of these subtle signals and the information they carry.

Day 13: You will reflect on the fact that inner stability is something we need to seek and nurture.

Day 14: You will focus on the good things you already have in your life.

All these practices of reflecting are intended to help you become aware and acknowledge your inner experiences instead of ignoring or dismissing them. When we reflect on our experiences with genuine curiosity and without judgment, we become more attuned to our needs, allowing us to recognize them and take appropriate action to meet them.

DAY 8

What's my attachment style?

"You can't understand me without understanding where I was created."

Morgan Freeman

Today's focus is on finding out what your attachment style is. During the first part of this book, we learned about the profound influence our attachment style has on our quality of life, so identifying your attachment style is a big first step toward a better understanding of your own self. Also, knowing your attachment style, especially in the case of an insecure attachment, can empower you to take intentional steps toward earned security.

Today, you might discover you have an insecure attachment style, which may bring up mixed emotions. You might experience sadness about the difficulties you had to face throughout your life due to your early environment. You might feel anger or disappointment toward those who hurt you instead of loving and caring for you. You might feel vulnerable or worried about how your attachment may continue to affect you in the future. You might feel shame about your attachment style, viewing it as a flaw of character rather than for what it is: a model of the world shaped by the environment you were raised in. You might also feel a sense of frustration for how profoundly your past continues to influence your present, or you might feel hopeless, unable to see how things could ever change for you.

On the other hand, you might experience a sense of relief and validation, understanding that the struggles you have been experiencing are not simply your fault but rather a reflection of your early childhood environment. You might feel empathy toward your own self, perhaps feeling compassion for all the difficult experiences you went through that were rooted in your attachment style. You might feel hopeful or motivated to take intentional steps toward earned security and developing healthier relationships. You might even decide to start a therapeutic process to help you gain a deeper understanding of your life's narrative and its profound influence on your patterns of thinking, emotions, interactions, and behaviors. Regardless of your experience, remember that although your attachment style is stable, it is not fixed.

Learning about your attachment style could unlock the potential to change the trajectory of your life for the better. It can provide you with valuable insights about your needs, fears, and behaviors. It can also help you better understand the patterns of interactions with others and the relationship you have with your own self. The sooner you identify your attachment style, especially in the case of an insecure attachment, the sooner you can move toward earned security. Knowing the benefits of having a secure attachment can be a source of motivation for everyone to reflect upon one's own attachment style and take steps in the direction of developing secure relationships.

Experiential activity

I invite you to take out your journal and a pen and find a quiet space where you can be comfortable and free from distractions. The first part of today's activity is identifying your attachment style. Then, for the second part, there will be several prompts for reflection. After each prompt, I invite you to close your eyes for a few moments, allowing yourself to reflect on your answers. There is no right or wrong way to answer the guiding prompts, so allow yourself to engage with the prompts freely and without any restrictions. Before you start, take a few deep breaths, letting go of any unnecessary tension in your body.

First, take the Relationship Structure Questionnaire, a self-assessment tool developed by Dr. Chris Fraley that measures adult attachment styles across relationships. You can find it online at https://www.web-research-design. net/cgi-bin/crq/crq.pl or by typing "relationship structure questionnaire by Dr. Chris Fraley" into your internet search engine. It usually takes between five and ten minutes to complete. This questionnaire is designed to help you learn more about the way you mentally represent important people in your life. For that reason, it asks questions about your parents, your romantic partner, and your friends. After you answer all the questions and submit your responses, you will receive a summary describing how your mind organizes these relationships.

After reading your results, follow the prompts below to reflect on how your attachment style is influencing the way you relate to yourself and others, particularly in close relationships. Reflecting on your attachment style can help you identify areas where you might need healing or growth. It might also bring warm feelings of empathy for your own self and others, recognizing that we all act or react in ways that are deeply rooted in our history and unmet emotional needs. Being aware and reflecting on your attachment style can lead to more mindful interactions, and it can help you make more intentional choices that align with your authentic desire for love and meaningful connections.

As you reflect on all the things listed below, gently remind yourself that although an attachment style is stable, it is not fixed. Rather, it is a dynamic dimension of life that can always evolve and transform.

- What is my emotional reaction as I'm learning about my attachment style? Do I feel relief, surprise, confusion, or perhaps even resistance to what I am discovering? Does it make me feel vulnerable, validated, or frustrated with certain aspects of myself?

- Which are the moments in my relationships where my attachment style played a significant role, either positively or negatively?

- How could understanding my attachment style change the way I relate to myself? For example, could I be more self-compassionate or motivated to know more after learning about it?

- What role can self-compassion play in changing my attachment patterns?

- How can I be kinder and more understanding toward myself when I experience insecurity in my relationships?

- How can I communicate my attachment needs to others? (Reflect on ways you can express your attachment style to partners, friends, or loved ones so they can better understand and support you.)

- What steps can I take to develop security within my relationships? (Reflect on practices or behaviors that might help you feel more confident and secure in your relationships.)

DAY 9

Permission to feel

*"The curious paradox is that when I accept myself, just as I am,
then I can change."*

Dr. Carl Rogers

Acknowledging and reflecting on physical sensations, thoughts, and emotions are powerful ways to understand our experiences, especially in challenging situations. It allows us to gain insight into the underlying causes of our distress and understand our physical and emotional needs. This insight can then help us take the necessary steps to alleviate the pain instead of creating unnecessary suffering by resisting it.

Pain and discomfort are inevitable parts of being alive. Regardless of who we are or what we do, we experience various degrees of pain as we go through life. Although pain is part of life, and we can't avoid it, we can definitely avoid suffering. You see, suffering arises out of resistance to pain. Resisting pain is a refusal to accept the present reality, which adds unnecessary physical, mental, and emotional strain as we fight against what is happening rather than allowing ourselves to fully feel it. When we try to avoid or wish the pain away, or become frustrated for feeling pain, we amplify the distress, rather than alleviating it. This extra layer of distress is created by resistance, not the pain itself.

In contrast, when we accept pain as part of our existence, acknowledge it, and allow ourselves to feel it, we stop fighting against it. This acceptance doesn't mean we like the pain or that we want it to last forever; it just allows the pain to exist without adding any extra weight of mental or emotional resistance. Acceptance of pain as a feature of our reality can also be a source of self-compassion. By acknowledging our humanity, we acknowledge that we, like all human beings, experience pain, which is not a sign of weakness or that something is wrong with us—it only means we are human. This acknowledgment then creates space for the same understanding, kindness, and support for oneself that we would offer to anyone in a similar situation.

As you move through the journey of self-regulation, you will encounter difficult sensations in your body, negative thoughts, and unpleasant emotions you might want to avoid, ignore, or suppress. When this happens, I invite you to give yourself permission to feel all these sensations and emotions with empathy, patience, and understanding. Being present with yourself in difficult situations without judgment and resistance is one of the deepest forms of care you can offer yourself.

Experiential activity

For today's practice, I invite you to take out your journal and a pen and find a quiet space where you can be comfortable and without distractions. The first part of today's practice is focused on accurately identifying and labeling your emotional experience. Then, for the second part, the focus will be on identifying the difference between discomfort and suffering.

There will be several prompts for reflection, and after each prompt, I invite you to close your eyes for a few moments, allowing yourself to reflect on your answers. There is no right or wrong way to answer the guiding prompts, so allow yourself to engage with the prompts freely and without any restrictions. Before you start, take a few deep breaths, letting go of any unnecessary tension in your body.

Name it to tame it

"Name it to tame it,"a term coined by Dr. Daniel J. Siegel, refers to the process of identifying and labeling emotions in order to better understand and regulate them. By labeling our emotions, we create a sense of distance from them instead of identifying with or being consumed by them. As you go through your day, I invite you to notice your emotions and try to name them as accurately as possible. So instead of saying, "I am not feeling good," "Something's wrong," "I'm having a good day," or "I feel good," take a moment and name the feeling with as much accuracy as possible. For example, instead of saying, "Something is wrong," you could say, "I feel anger," "I feel worried," "I feel sad." Instead of saying, "I'm having a good day," you could say, "I feel joy," "I feel grateful," "I feel excited."

As much as we enjoy pleasant emotions, we dislike unpleasant ones, and we tend to avoid or ignore them. My invitation to you today is to start observing your experiences and naming them without any judgment. What you will notice is that by accurately labeling your emotions, such as "I feel worried" or "I feel embarrassed," you'll gain a better understanding of your experiences and become less overwhelmed by them. Why? Because distinguishing between feeling "irritated," "angry," or "disappointed" versus feeling "sad" not only gives you clarity about your inner experience but also about what you might need in that moment.

To start the "name it to tame it" process, I invite you to use the list below and highlight all the emotions you have felt today since the moment you opened your eyes. Take your time with this; there is no need to rush it. Then, as you go on with your day, allow yourself to pause and name both the pleasant and unpleasant emotions you might experience in that moment.

Admiration	Euphoria	Nostalgia
Affection	Excitement	Optimism
Alienation	Fear	Panic
Amusement	Frustration	Peace
Anger	Gratification	Pessimism
Anxiety	Gratitude	Playfulness
Awe	Grief	Powerlessness
Bliss	Guilt	Pride
Calm	Happiness	Regret
Compassion	Hate	Rejection
Contentment	Hope	Relief
Delight	Hopelessness	Resentment
Despair	Humiliation	Sadness
Disappointment	Hurt	Satisfaction
Discomfort	Inspiration	Serendipity
Disgust	Insecurity	Serenity
Distrust	Irritation	Shame
Eagerness	Isolation	Shyness
Elation	Jealousy	Tenderness
Embarrassment	Joy	Trust
Empathy	Loneliness	Wonder
Envy	Love	Worry

Am I feeling discomfort, or am I suffering?

We can experience discomfort without suffering, but we cannot experience suffering without discomfort. The question is, how do we tell the difference between the two? This exercise will help you go through the process of differentiating between them. For the purpose of this exercise, I invite you to recall a recent situation when you experienced mild to moderate discomfort—for example, a time when you were waiting in a long line, felt nervous before speaking in front of an audience, after a minor conflict with a loved one, or when doing something you didn't enjoy such as a chore or task. Once you've recalled the situation, take out your journal and write down the answers to the following questions:

What was I thinking or saying?

- Signs of accepting the situation: *I don't like this, but I can handle it. This is uncomfortable, but it's temporary. It's okay to feel this way. This is part of the process. It's not easy, but I can take it one step at a time. This is hard, but I can go through it. I'm learning from this experience.*

- Signs of fighting against the situation: *Why is this happening to me? This shouldn't be happening. I shouldn't feel this way. Why do I always have to do this? I shouldn't have to do this. This is stupid. I don't want to do this. This is not fair.*

What was I feeling?

- Signs of accepting the situation: *empathy, compassion, acceptance, calmness, hope, patience, courage, trust, forgiveness.*

- Signs of fighting against the situation: *body tension, tightness in your stomach, self-doubt, helplessness, anxiety, impatience, fear, frustration, worry, irritability.*

What was I doing?

- Signs of accepting the situation: *took deep breaths, focused on the things I could control, sought support from others, expressed myself calmly, soothed myself with gentle or supportive touch.*

- Signs of fighting against the situation: *clenched my fists and jaw, blamed myself or others, tried to escape or avoid the situation, overworked, drank*

> *alcohol or used substances, fidgeted, was breathing rapidly or shallowly, avoided eye contact.*

Any time you experience a challenging situation, pause and take notice of the sensations in your body, your thoughts, and emotions. Then take a moment to ask yourself whether what you are experiencing is just discomfort or whether there is added pain created by resistance. If you notice any signs of resistance, use the anchoring strategies you learned during the first seven days of this journey to release the grip of resistance, if only for a moment.

DAY 10

The wisdom from within: My inner guide

"We all have that inner voice that is wise, even if we don't always follow it. It's that voice I'm trying to listen to."

Ray LaMontagne

Whether we are aware of it or not, there is great wisdom that lies within each of us, rooted in our true essence, inner values, and deepest desires. This wisdom from within stems from our authentic self, which is always there to guide us in making decisions that honor our true self. When we allow ourselves to be guided by inner wisdom, we navigate life with more clarity, ease, and purpose.

Oftentimes, we refer to inner wisdom as conscience, intuition, gut feeling, or a deep sense of knowing, and it can be recognized as a sense of calmness, clarity, ease, warmth, openness, vitality, peace, certainty, insight, optimism, or gratitude. At all times and in any circumstance, we can access our inner wisdom by paying attention to our physical sensations, internal dialogue, and emotions. Today's practice, adapted from the work of Dr. Paul Gilbert, will focus on the experience of identifying the physical cues, thoughts, and emotions associated with it.

Experiential activity

For today's practice, I invite you to take out your journal and a pen and find a quiet space where you can be comfortable and free from interruptions. There will be several prompts for reflection, and after each prompt, I invite you to close your eyes for a few moments, allowing yourself to experience any sensations, images, thoughts, or emotions that might come to you. There is no right or wrong way to answer the guiding prompts, so please allow your inner wisdom to flow freely through your answers. When you are ready, take a few deep breaths, allowing your body to relax and your attention to move inward.

Now imagine you are in a peaceful setting where you feel safe and comfortable. This could be a house or a room in a house; somewhere in nature, such as a garden, a tranquil beach, a forest meadow, a mountain peak; or wherever feels peaceful to you. Take a few moments to fully visualize this place. What does it look like? What do you hear, smell, and feel around you? How does your body feel in this environment? Close your eyes for a few moments, letting yourself enjoy the comfort of this space, and open them again when you are ready to describe this location in a few words in your journal.

Now imagine someone approaching you in this peaceful place. It is a wise being who embodies the qualities of patience, strength, and unconditional love, and whose presence feels warm and kind. This could be a human, such as a wise teacher or a grandparent. It could also be an animal or a supernatural form like a spiritual being, a beam of light, or a gentle presence that you can only feel. This being is a friend that cares deeply about you, wants you to be well, and supports you unconditionally. Be however you naturally feel most comfortable and take some time to enjoy the presence of this friend. If it feels good, close your eyes for a few moments, allowing yourself to fully experience any sensations and emotions that might arise in their presence. Then, when you are ready, open your eyes and write down your experience.

This gentle friend knows you well, knows your fears and struggles, your wishes and desires, and holds the answers to all the questions you ever wanted to know, so you can talk about anything you want with this friend. This wise and compassionate friend listens attentively to everything you have to say, not only for the words you are saying but also for the true meaning behind them. If there are no words you want to share, take a few moments and just continue to be in the presence of your friend.

Before leaving the peaceful place, this wise friend wants to tell you something you need to hear right now in your life, so listen to what they are telling you. The message could come in the form of words, but it might also appear as an image, an insight, or a feeling. Then, when you are ready, open your eyes and write down the message you received.

As your friend is leaving your peaceful place, take a moment to reflect on their wise, gentle presence and all the answers, images, or words you've just experienced. Your friend carried wisdom, kindness, gentleness, understanding, compassion, and unconditional love. This friend is actually part of you, and all the qualities of this friend are part of your inner being. The message you received came from that part of yourself that knows your heart and your fears and is always there for you, without judgment and with unconditional love. Your inner wisdom is gentle, understanding, and compassionate and wants you to be well and live without any unnecessary suffering. Whenever you need guidance, your inner wisdom is available to you.

DAY 11

The harsh judgment from within:
My inner critic

"What is this self inside us, this silent observer, severe and speechless critic, who can terrorize us and urge us on to futile activity, and in the end judge us still more severely for the errors into which his own reproaches drove us?"

T.S. Eliot

Living in society involves following rules, meeting expectations, and delivering on demands. Failure to do so can be followed by various degrees of consequences, from disapproval to harsh criticism, and even rejection. In order to avoid possible painful consequences, we develop an internal way of monitoring that we are doing "the right things," which helps us not only survive but also thrive in society.

There is nothing wrong with having expectations, rules, and demands. In fact, they create the structure and predictability we need to navigate life with more ease. But what if our early environment was critical and judgmental, and the rules, expectations, and demands were too rigid and unrealistic? In that case, it is likely we developed an internal monitoring process that is also critical and judgmental, and internal rules, expectations, and demands that might be too rigid and unrealistic—in other words, an inner voice that continuously questions us, challenging our abilities and decisions. In some cases, this voice becomes undermining and insulting in a harsh and persistent way. Simply put, we develop an inner critic.

We tend to use self-criticism as a voice of reason and motivation to help us improve by constantly pointing out our flaws and mistakes. We believe it can protect us from failure and embarrassment by continuously assessing and warning us about our decisions, actions, and behavior, or by comparing ourselves to others and evaluating our worth or adequacy. Because we assign a protective value to this voice, we accept it as the voice of truth that urges us to do what's "right" and always make the "right" decisions. But what if this voice is harming us more than helping us?

The focus of today's practice is to create space to reflect on our inner critical voice, its origins, and whether this voice is protecting or hurting us.

Experiential activity

I invite you to take out your journal and a pen and find a quiet space where you can be comfortable and free from interruptions. There will be several prompts for reflection, and after each prompt, I invite you to close your eyes for a few moments, allowing yourself to experience any sensations, images, thoughts, or emotions that might arise. There is no right or wrong way to answer the guiding prompts, so please let your answers flow freely through your writing. When you are ready, take a few deep breaths, allowing your body to relax and your attention to move inward.

Now I invite you to think of a recent difficulty you've been through but that has been resolved now. For the purpose of today's activity, I invite you to choose a mild to moderate situation, such as a disagreement with a friend, missing an important deadline, having to make an important decision, difficulty maintaining healthy eating habits, or struggling to maintain a consistent exercise routine. Take a few moments to think of this struggle, and when you are ready, describe it in your journal. If, at any point, thinking about it becomes overwhelming, use an anchoring strategy to ground yourself in the present moment, or completely disengage from the exercise.

Next, I invite you to take a deep breath in, followed by a long exhale, and then close your eyes for a few moments and recall the internal dialogue you were having during that time of struggle. Was this internal dialogue supportive and kind, such as:

- *It's okay to feel this way.*

- *I've been through tough times before, and I got through them.*

- *I'm doing the best I can right now.*

- *This feeling is temporary, and it will pass.*

- *I am worthy of kindness and compassion.*

- *I don't have to have all the answers right now.*

- *I can take this one step at a time.*

Or was your internal dialogue critical, insulting, and undermining, such as:

- *I am so stupid.*

- *I should be stronger than this.*

- *Everyone else has their life together. What's wrong with me?*

- *I don't deserve to be happy.*

- *I can't do anything right.*

- *I'll never be good enough.*

- *I'm just a burden to everyone around me...?*

In your journal describe your internal dialogue.

Now I invite you to take a deep breath in, followed by a long exhale. If your internal dialogue was supportive and caring, continue to remind yourself that struggles are part of life, and we all do the best we can to overcome them. However, if your internal dialogue was critical, insulting, and undermining, please take a moment to acknowledge this harsh criticism.

With curiosity, turn your attention to this critical voice and see whether its intention is to protect you or to put you down. If the intention is to protect you, I invite you to use the voice of your inner wisdom to thank this critical voice and let it know it isn't helping you right now. On the contrary, it is hurting you. You can say things like, *I know you want to protect me, but your harshness is not helping me right now. If anything, it hurts me,* or *Thank you for your intention to protect me, but I've got this. You can rest now.*

If the critical voice is there to put you down, turn up the gentle voice of your inner wisdom to protect you from this harsh voice. Your inner wisdom is likely to say things like, *This is a difficult moment for me, and in difficult times I can rely on things that bring me comfort,* or *I am deserving of love and care just like any other human being.* You can also use gestures of self-compassion to soothe the effects of the harsh criticism or anchor in the things you know feel good to you.

Most times, we listen to the harsh judgment from within without questioning it. We are so accustomed to this voice that we rarely pause and reflect on where this voice is coming from, how it developed, and whether this voice might be harming us more than helping us. The more we practice questioning, quieting, and soothing the effects of the inner critic, the more space we create for the gentle voice of inner wisdom to be heard. We might not always be able to completely silence the inner critic, but at least we can turn its volume down.

DAY 12

How do I know when I'm dysregulated?

*"Until you make the unconscious conscious, it will direct your life,
and you will call it fate."*

Dr. Carl Jung

Cues such as a clenched jaw, a faster heartbeat, a sense of restlessness, irritability, fatigue, a headache, scattered thoughts, and feeling distracted or inattentive are all early signs that we are out of balance. These subtle signals could mean the body budget is running on a deficit; we might be caught in loops of overthinking or experience unwanted emotions. Awareness of these early signs is the first step toward identifying the source of dysregulation, which opens the opportunity to intervene before we become fully dysregulated.

Oftentimes, we ignore or minimize early signals of distress with the hope they might go away. This can lead to negative long-term consequences, such as physical illness, intrusive thoughts, emotional outbursts, or inappropriate behavior, so acknowledging and reflecting on these early indicators could save us a great deal of struggle. For that reason, today we will experience the process of identifying early signs of dysregulation and reflect on their source and the information they carry.

Experiential activity

For today's practice, I invite you to take out your journal and a pen and find a quiet space where you can be comfortable and free of distractions. There will be several prompts for reflection, and after each prompt, I invite you to close your eyes for a few moments, allowing yourself to reflect on your answers. There is no right or wrong way to answer the guiding prompts, so allow yourself to engage with them freely and without any restrictions. Before you start, take a few deep breaths, letting go of any unnecessary tension in your body.

When you are ready, I invite you to think of a struggle you have been through recently. For the purpose of today's activity, think of a mild to moderate struggle, not something big or too upsetting—for example, feeling unappreciated for something you've done, being interrupted when you were trying to express something important, missing a deadline, your words were taken the wrong way, you forgot an important date, or felt left out. Take a few moments to think about this struggle, and once you have it clear in your mind, write down your answers to the prompts below.

- When I was experiencing the struggle, what I felt in my body was… *[e.g., tense muscles, teary eyes, a lump in my throat, increased heart rate, restlessness, a knot in my stomach, tightness in my chest, a clenched jaw, headache, hot ears, shaking body]*

- When I was experiencing the struggle, I was thinking… *[e.g., I always mess up. It's not that big of a deal. I'm such an idiot. Get it together. I am going to do better next time. Everyone makes mistakes. No one likes me. They are making fun of me.]*

- When I was experiencing the struggle, I was feeling… *[e.g., irritated, angry, sad, worried, rejected, anxious]*

- When I was experiencing the struggle, my behavior was… *[e.g., defensive, reactive, impulsive, on the verge of exploding, withdrawn]*

- When I was experiencing the struggle, my words toward others were… *[e.g., unkind, mean, minimal, as usual, like nothing happened, apologetic]*

As you are finishing today's activity, take a moment to reflect on the importance of identifying and acknowledging the early signals of dysregulation. Rather than ignoring or suppressing these signs, we can use them to identify their root cause and intervene in ways that are beneficial for us.

DAY 13

How do I know when I'm balanced?

"To experience embodied awareness, take notice of the underlying sensations that actually inform you about how you feel."

Dr. Peter A. Levine

When was the last time you paused to acknowledge your body feeling good, without any discomfort or pain? Or noticed your internal dialogue being calm and grounded? When was the last time you enjoyed the deep quiet within you, when your emotions were not running the show? Although we all strive for balance, we rarely pause to acknowledge and savor the moments when things go well for us. Mostly, we tend to take our state of balance for granted, treating it as a given, like something we are entitled to. It's only when faced with a difficult situation, illness, or a chronic disease that we start to appreciate the quiet harmony of stability. A state of balance is more than just feeling good; it is an indication that we feel safe and connected and our body has the necessary resources to function at its optimal level.

Internal equilibrium is available to us. However, it is not something that just happens to us but rather something we need to seek and nurture. It is an ongoing and fluid process that we have to actively maintain. And just like any other process, this one starts with awareness, too. So how do we know when we are in a state of balance? And what are the cues telling us that we are balanced? What does a state of balance look like? Today's focus is on answering these questions by reflecting on the physical sensations, thoughts, emotions, and behaviors connected to the sense of balance.

Experiential activity

For today's practice, I invite you to take out your journal and a pen and find a quiet space in which you can be comfortable and without distractions. There will be several prompts for reflection, and after each prompt, I invite you to close your eyes for a few moments, allowing yourself to reflect on your answers. There is no right or wrong way to answer the guiding prompts, so allow your answers to be led by your experience. Before you start, take a few deep breaths, letting go of any unnecessary tension in your body.

When you are ready, I invite you to recall a peaceful time in your life. It could be a time when you felt safe and connected and everything seemed to fall into place, or just an uneventful time with no big highs or lows and no pressing challenges to overcome. Think of a time when you felt a sense of ease and stability. This time in your life doesn't have to be a lengthy period. It could be a deep relaxing breath that brings the mind to stillness, the comfort of a warm blanket on a Sunday morning while still in bed, a quiet moment of appreciation that brings serenity and ease, a day with time to rest, with no obligations or external pressure to accomplish anything, or a weekend free to follow your own rhythm.

Take a few moments to think about this peaceful time in your life, and if it feels good, you can close your eyes, allowing yourself to get immersed in the memory of that time. Once you have the memory clear in your mind, write down the answers to the prompts below. As you are writing your answers, I invite you to pause and savor any feel-good sensations, thoughts, or emotions that might arise.

- When I was experiencing the peaceful time, what I felt in my body was… *[e.g., relaxed muscles, breathing deeply and easily, warm hands, a light and comfortable belly, effortless movement]*

- When I was experiencing the peaceful time, I was thinking… *[e.g., Life is good right now. This feels really good. I'm really enjoying this moment. I am so lucky. I feel so relaxed. I could stay like this forever.]*

- When I was experiencing the peaceful time, I was feeling… *[e.g., happy, comfortable, content, thankful]*

- When I was experiencing the peaceful time, my behavior was… *[e.g., engaging, supportive, gentle, non-defensive]*

- When I was experiencing the peaceful time, my words were… *[e.g., kind, positive, supportive, caring, playful]*

As you are finishing today's activity, take a moment to reflect on one thing you could do every day to increase your state of balance.

DAY 14

The good things that are already happening: What am I grateful for?

"I set off a gratitude bomb in my journal yesterday. Science says that gratitude is good for you. Like, REALLY good for you."

Elizabeth Gilbert

Did you know that we, human beings, are wired to scan for danger? This wiring is deeply rooted in our evolution, and it helps us survive by either avoiding or responding to danger before it becomes life-threatening. In science, this scan for danger is called **negativity bias**, meaning that we tend to pay more attention to the negative experiences than the positive ones. We are also more likely to remember unpleasant experiences than pleasant ones. For instance, we can be given several pieces of positive feedback and quickly forget them, but when we receive one criticism, we might ruminate on it for days or even longer. This radar for negativity has many adaptive benefits, helping us avoid risks and learn from our mistakes. However, it can also interfere with seeing the good things that are happening in our life. For this reason, today we will counterbalance the natural tendency toward negativity by focusing on what is already going well and expressing gratitude for all those things. By doing this, we can rewire how we perceive ourselves and the world.

Experiential activity

For today's practice, I invite you to take out your journal and a pen and find a quiet space in which you can be comfortable and without distractions. Before you start, take a few deep breaths, letting go of any unnecessary tension in your body.

When you are ready, I invite you to start writing down all the things you are grateful for today. They can range from small things, such as the sound of birds, the beauty of a sunset, or the smell of blooming flowers, to big things, such as your health, your eyes that help you navigate the world, or the good people who love and support you. Write down all the things you are grateful for, no matter how big or small. The purpose of this experience is not to search for big accomplishments that you are proud of but rather look for all the small things within and around you that bring you pleasant feelings.

As you write down the things you are grateful for, slow down and allow yourself to savor each moment, letting the gratitude permeate every cell of your body. Then, as you continue your journey of self-regulation, set your intention to write three things each day that you are grateful for.

DAYS 15–21

Transforming: Create New Predictions

"Peace must first be developed within an individual."

Dalai Lama

For the final seven days of your journey to self-regulation, you will be focusing on the process of **transforming**—you will take intentional steps to create new positive experiences, providing your brain with the opportunity to create new predictions for the future.

Day 15: You will practice intentionally directing and sustaining attention so you can then use it to focus on what matters most to you.

Day 16: You will experience four strategies to create new experiences of ease and comfort in your body that can help you maintain a composed attitude, even when faced with discomfort.

Day 17: You will focus on cultivating balanced thinking through the process of bringing thoughts into your awareness, examining them, and responding to them in real time in ways that serve you best.

Day 18: You will practice the process of accurately identifying and labeling your emotions while differentiating between past and current experiences.

Day 19: You will give yourself overt permission to choose what feels good so your brain can create new predictions that increase the quality of your daily life.

Day 20: You will turn your attention inward again, and with genuine care you will create space for awareness of all physical, mental, and emotional states, without any intention to change anything.

Day 21: You will focus on slowing down by doing less and *being* more, moving at a pace that allows you to savor life rather than just moving through it.

All these practices of transforming are intended to open you up to new experiences of curiosity, clarity, connection, gratitude, inspiration, conscious action, and authentic living. By taking intentional steps in the process of transforming, we create a cycle of positive experiences that feed on each other—pleasant experiences will create positive predictions, which will lead to more pleasant experiences, eventually creating a pleasant life. Basically, by intentionally creating pleasant experiences, we thoughtfully shape the life we desire.

DAY 15

Regulating attention

"The difference between misery and happiness depends on
what we do with our attention."

Sharon Salzberg

Have you ever picked up your phone when you received a notification, been distracted by colorful products in a store, or found yourself reading random posts on social media? If you did, your attention was successfully stolen from you. We are continuously bombarded with information and situations competing for our attention: emails, texts, phone calls, family, friends, co-workers, projects, deadlines, bills, radio, TV, social media, shiny advertisements, conflicts, or internal dialogues—all requiring our attention. By the end of the day, we are often left feeling drained and as if we are running on autopilot.

Besides the external environment, our attention can also get sucked into deep memory lines of past hurts and unresolved situations, or become lost creating future possibilities and attempting to control what is yet to come. Have you ever had internal arguments with people who are not even in your life anymore? Have you ever re-lived painful situations over and over again with the same intensity as if they were happening right now? Have you ever run virtual scenarios of the future in your mind? If you did, you spent precious moments on a past that cannot be changed and a future that you can't really predict.

Between all these internal and external stimuli competing for and stealing our attention, we are often left with no space to choose what really matters to us. Our biology is such that we can only focus our attention on one thing at a time. Meaning, if we are paying attention to a conversation, we can't be paying attention to what's on TV, what happened yesterday, or what will happen tomorrow. Of course, we can rapidly shift our attention from one thing to another, giving us the illusion that we are simultaneously focusing on more than one thing at a time. In fact, what happens is that each time we shift our attention between things, we interrupt the flow of information. For example, when you are in the middle of a conversation and your mind starts to wander to what you should wear tomorrow, you are missing part of the conversation while mentally sorting through your closet. Sometimes, you can quickly shift your attention back to the discussion, nod in agreement to whatever the person in front of you is saying, and catch up with the conversation. However, if the person asks a question in the middle of your mind-wandering, your lack of attention becomes evident because you missed the context of the question while running virtual scenarios in your mind.

Being in charge of our attention is important because it is the gateway to everything we experience, shaping our actions, thoughts, and emotions, which directly influence our wellbeing. The more we can intentionally direct our attention, the more we can shape our reality and lead a life that aligns with our values and goals. We don't have to be at the mercy of internal and external distractions. As a matter of fact, we can intentionally direct our attention on things that make us feel at ease, positive, or grateful. We can intentionally focus our attention on what matters most to us, whether it's a task, a relationship, or personal growth.

Experiential activity

During today's practice, you will go through the experience of maintaining focused attention for one minute. It is up to you what you focus on. You could close your eyes and focus your attention on your breathing, feeling the natural rhythm of your chest moving up and down with each inhale and exhale or feeling the air moving in and out through your nostrils. Alternatively, you could focus your attention on a sound already present in your environment, such as the hum of the refrigerator or air conditioner. Or you might choose to keep your eyes open and focus on an object in front of you. You could also focus your attention on the sense of touch, feeling your body touching the surface you are sitting on, your clothes touching your skin, or skin touching skin. You might choose to pay attention to the sense of smell or taste. Whatever you choose to focus your attention on, do that for a whole minute.

Set an alarm for one minute and pay attention to one thing only. If the alarm goes off and you feel as if you could have carried on for two, five, ten, or even more minutes, do so. The aim here is to expand your capacity to direct and sustain your attention despite the internal and external stimuli. If, during this exercise, you notice your mind starting to wander, simply redirect your attention to the original point of focus.

I invite you to continue with this practice every day and grow it over time. The practice of holding attention steadily on one thing will help you not only increase your capacity for sustained attention but also notice where your mind is wandering and what your body is experiencing. You can use this practice in the morning after you wake up, at lunch, in the evening, or any other time that works for you. You might notice it is easier to practice in the morning than in the afternoon, when the mind gets tired and, as a result, sustaining attention becomes more challenging.

Day 16

Regulating the body

*"Your body is your temple. You do your body good,
your body will do you good."*

Floyd Mayweather Jr.

If you've ever experienced a fever, chills, headaches, or pain in your body, you'll know discomfort in the body shadows all aspects of life. So, if wellbeing is the goal, then caring for our body is non-negotiable and needs to be at the top of our priority list. If we want to function efficiently and remain adaptable to both internal and external changes, we need the foundation of a well-functioning body. Just like we can't build a roof without the structure of a house, we can't build wellbeing without a healthy body.

The body is the vessel that contains our life, so our quality of life is contingent on the wellbeing of our body. Our body sets the tone for all aspects of our life, including mental, emotional, relational, and professional wellbeing. If the body is not functioning properly and is running on a deficit, everything else will crumble.

Human bodies exist along a spectrum—some people experience full physical function, while others live with varying degrees of physical disability. Whatever your situation, it's important to do what you can within your own limits to care for and support your body. Eating nutritious food, drinking enough water, getting adequate sleep, and exercising need to be part of our daily routine. There is no magic wand, no pill, or meditation practice that can replace these necessary elements that support the functioning of the body. Once these basics are provided, we can further support the body with intentional practices that help us regain or maintain its balance during difficult situations. Targeted support can lessen the impact of various threats on the body but also provide a sense of ease.

Today's focus is to learn and experience strategies we can implement when the regulated state of the body is threatened by various factors, such as high demands, increased stress, or danger. These strategies can buffer the negative impact of various stressors and modulate the intensity of discomfort they create in our body. They can also prevent the body from getting out of sync and effectively adapt to both internal changes and the demands of the environment. By creating new experiences of ease and comfort in our body during difficult situations, we can help the brain create new and more adaptive predictions in the future.

Experiential activity

Fuel your body

Before you start, I invite you to reflect on whether you are providing your body with the necessary elements for proper functioning. The checklist below is intended to help you identify if any of these basic elements are missing from your routine. I invite you to use this list as a tool for awareness and not one for judgment. We all know that habits and the demands of life can affect the way we eat, how much we sleep, and whether we move our body. So, as you go over the list below, if you find you are falling short in any of the listed areas, please be gentle with yourself. Take note of what is missing, do it without judgment, and set an intention to take steps that could help you improve in that area. Be kind to yourself—there is a first step in every journey.

- ☐ Nutritious food (e.g., meat, vegetables, fruit)

- ☐ Adequate amount of water (e.g., about 68 fl oz / 2 liters a day)

- ☐ Enough sleep (e.g., 7–9 hours of sleep a night)

- ☐ Exercise (e.g., walking, running, lifting, yoga, dancing)

Support your body to create new predictions

Today, you will learn and practice four powerful strategies that can transform your experiences in real time from unpleasant to pleasant ones. I will also introduce you to the most effective way to practice regulating your body. These practices show us we can remain collected, even when faced with discomfort. So I invite you to take your time with each of them, allowing yourself to get immersed in the experience of each practice.

Panoramic vision

Have you ever wondered why looking up at the sky, taking in the view from a mountain peak, or looking over a wide-open lake or ocean can feel so peaceful? The answer lies in our biology. Our eyes are directly connected to our autonomic nervous system, and when we look at panoramic views, the part that helps our body relax gets activated instantly.

We can naturally draw our gaze into panoramic vision, either by looking at the horizon or by softening our gaze. You might not always have access to the open sky, the ocean, or a mountain peak to help you achieve panoramic vision, but you can still activate it by finding a fixed spot in your environment to soften your gaze in an unfocused way. Meditators are known to use the soft gaze on a fixed point, such as a candlelight, to achieve a state of relaxation.

Let's try it now. Find a fixed spot in your environment—like a pen, a desk, or a dot in the carpet—allowing your gaze to become unfocused for a few moments. When your gaze becomes unfocused, you can also see the objects in your peripheral vision, to the left and right. One of the immediate signs of relaxation is a big yawn, which you will experience almost immediately. Enjoy the yawn. It always feels good.

Patterns of breathing

Feeling low and want to increase your energy? Make sure your inhales are longer than your exhales. Feeling worried, tense, or stressed and want to help your body relax? Make sure your exhales are longer than your inhales. Just like with panoramic vision, the answer to why various patterns of breathing work lies in our biology. The communication between the body and the brain, guided by the breath, can speed our heart rate up or down depending on what breathing pattern we choose.

Based on your immediate needs, use the four patterns of breathing you learned about during the second day of this journey: physiological sigh, relaxing, energizing, or coherent breathing.

Sitting meditation

Sitting meditation is one of the most powerful ways to practice regulating your body. This practice highlights how frequently we act on the impulse to relieve discomfort in our body without being aware of it. If you are familiar with the practice of sitting meditation, you already know its power, and if you haven't come across it before, you are about to find out its value.

For this practice, I invite you to find a quiet space without any distractions and get in a comfortable position in which you can be still for at least five minutes. You might want to sit comfortably on a chair or lie down on a bed, couch, or the floor. During this time of complete stillness, I invite you to take the role of an observer and notice any thoughts, sensations, or impulses that arise within you at any given moment. Observe your experience without any judgment and notice if you have any urges to change what you are experiencing.

Throughout this practice, I invite you to use your breath to anchor yourself in the present moment and to create ease within your body. Whenever you find yourself getting lost in your thoughts or striving for your experience to be something other than it is, take a deep breath in and drop back into your body. When you need to bring ease into certain areas of your body, relax your muscles and let go of any unnecessary tension you might be experiencing. You might become aware that when the body feels discomfort, the mind also struggles, and when the mind struggles, the body feels discomfort.

During this practice, you may experience unpleasant sensations in your body, such as itching, tingling, pain, or numbness, and you might feel the urge to move your body. If that happens, I invite you to notice that urge without acting on it and see what other experiences might arise from it. Of course, if your body is in a position that causes you pain, and adjusting your position is necessary, you can do it slowly and mindfully. However, if the discomfort is not related to the position you are in, see if you can observe your experience without acting on the impulse to move, but rather acknowledge it with empathy and compassion, letting your inner voice whisper, *This is a difficult moment for me. Discomfort is hard.*

You might also find yourself experiencing unpleasant thoughts like *I can't do this; I can't sit here doing nothing for five minutes; This is stupid; If I'm not moving, I will go crazy; My nose is itching, I need to scratch it; My leg hurts, I need to move it.* Whatever your thoughts are, notice them, and if you find yourself getting lost in them, gently return to your breath.

Practicing in this way for five minutes is a good place to start. However, if five minutes of stillness feels unbearable to you, start with one or two minutes. Over time, as you continue to practice, your ability to maintain stillness will increase significantly, allowing you to contain your experience for longer periods of time. The purpose of this practice isn't to become a professional meditator but to learn that you can take charge and contain whatever experience you might encounter.

This new experience of being in charge of your actions, rather than being at the mercy of your thoughts, sensations, or impulses, will become a new source of information for your brain's predictions. Think of the sitting meditation practice as training that increases your ability to maintain stability so you don't become overwhelmed by difficult situations. Just like a student studies for an exam, an athlete trains for a competition, and a performer rehearses for a big show, you can use the sitting meditation to prepare for life's challenges.

Move your body

Whenever you find yourself experiencing unpleasant thoughts, emotions, or physical sensations, get up and move. You can create new experiences, and therefore new predictions, by simply moving your body. Whether it is gentle stretching, taking a walk, dancing, yoga, or any other type of exercise, movement has the power to change your experience.

Change the location

Sometimes, all you need is to change the location to improve your experience. So get out of your bed, off your couch, out of your house, or move from wherever you are and go to a different location, perhaps another room, a coffee shop, a park, a library, or a friend's house.

DAY 17

Regulating your thoughts

"Our life is shaped by our mind, for we become what we think."

Buddha

Have you ever worried yourself sick playing out the worst-case scenarios in your head on repeat? Or have you ever believed you could do something, and then did it without questioning your ability? Thoughts play a fundamental role in shaping our reality, influencing nearly every aspect of our life including emotional states, physical reactions, the way we behave, how we interact with others, and, ultimately, the quality of our overall experiences. Thoughts are powerful tools for creation—they help us generate virtual realities that assist us in planning, achieving, and creating new possibilities. We can use our inner voice and mental images to think through challenges, make decisions, reflect on situations, and generate dialogues, speeches, and arguments. Thoughts are powerful, and like any powerful thing, they can help us or break us.

Our thoughts are influenced by everything we see, hear, and experience. The music, news, and the podcasts we listen to; the movies we watch; what we scroll through on social media; the books we read; and the people we spend time with all influence our daily thoughts. Over time, these daily thoughts become our beliefs, which ultimately become our life.

When our beliefs are shaped by pleasant and constructive thoughts of optimism, generosity, gratitude, and self-compassion, a sense of balance is fostered and supported. In contrast, when our beliefs are shaped by unpleasant or rigid thoughts, such as fear, doubt, perfectionism, pessimism, and blame, there is an increased likelihood of physical and emotional distress.

Today, you will be focusing on cultivating a balanced way of thinking. More specifically, you will experience the process of bringing your thoughts into awareness, examining them, and responding to them in real time in ways that serve you best. While you might not be able to control the initial thoughts as they arise, you can train yourself to change or stop negative mental loops by acknowledging and directing them toward more pleasant and empowering thoughts.

Experiential activity

For today's practice, I invite you to find a quiet space where you can be comfortable and free from distractions. This activity has four parts, each with a different prompt. After reading each prompt, I invite you to close your eyes for a few minutes and follow the prompt's instructions. Be mindful that you might experience increased discomfort during this experience, and if that happens, please use the anchoring strategies that work best for you. If your experience becomes too distressing, allow yourself to disengage from the activity and do something completely different and pleasant that you know brings you ease and comfort. There is no right or wrong way of going through this experience, so please engage in it in a way that works for you. Before you start, I invite you to take a few deep breaths, letting go of any unnecessary tension in your body.

Now, for the first part of this experience, I invite you to move your attention toward your thoughts. The intention here is not to focus on specific thoughts but rather to allow the flow of thoughts to enter your awareness. Imagine yourself being the observer of your own thought parade, watching each thought after another, without judgment and without following any specific thought, allowing each thought to come and go without holding on to any of them.

At first, you might find it difficult to be the observer of your own thoughts. You might find yourself experiencing a gap in your thoughts: *There are no thoughts for me to observe.* If that's your experience, don't worry—that is a thought in itself. Give yourself a couple of minutes to settle into this observer experience, allowing each thought to come and go without any restriction. If it helps, set an alarm for at least two minutes.

For the second part of this activity, I invite you to continue to watch your thoughts, but this time, notice where each thought is arising from. How does it appear in your awareness? How long does it stay there? And how does it leave your awareness? Is it sudden? Gradual? Once a thought appears, does it just stay there, or does it come and go? Again, give yourself a couple of minutes for this part of the exercise, and if you find it helpful, set an alarm for two minutes or for as long as you want to.

Next, for the third part of the activity, I invite you to pay attention to the quality of your thoughts. Are your thoughts pleasant or unpleasant? Are they fearful, critical, blaming, or are they forgiving, understanding, and hopeful? As you are observing your thought parade, with each thought entering and leaving your awareness, see if you can label them. For example, if you notice fearful thoughts, such as *What if I fail and everyone sees it?; Something bad is going to happen;* or *I won't finish the project in time*, say, "Fear." If you notice blaming thoughts, such as *If he hadn't made that mistake, I wouldn't be in this position; She always makes me upset;* or *It is my fault that we are always fighting*, say, "Blame." If you notice encouraging thoughts, such as *I am making progress even if it is slow; Everyone makes mistakes, and we can all learn from them;* or *This hard time will pass, just like everything else*, say, "Encouragement." Whatever thoughts you observe, label them instead of being caught in them. Give yourself a couple of minutes or more for this part of the exercise and set an alarm if you find it helpful.

Finally, for the fourth and final part of the exercise, I invite you to use two different strategies to help you respond to unpleasant thoughts when they arise. First, you can respond to your thoughts by using your kind and supportive inner voice. For example, if you notice critical, fearful, or blaming thoughts, you could tell yourself, *I notice this thought, but I don't have to engage with it; This is difficult, but I have faced challenges before and gotten through them; I make mistakes, but I am worthy of love and care; This is just a thought, it doesn't define who I am.*

Sometimes, the thoughts might be really harsh or intrusive, and the supportive inner voice might be aggressively shut down by them. If that happens, move your attention from your thoughts to something else—for example, your breathing, the sensation of clothing on your skin, or the soles of your feet on the ground. Use whatever anchoring method works best for you to move your attention away from your thoughts. This will help stop the negative loop of thoughts in that very moment. You can use this strategy any time you find yourself getting caught in unpleasant intrusive thoughts. The purpose of this radical approach is not to avoid unpleasant thoughts, as they are part of being human, but to break cycles of rumination that are more hurtful than helpful.

DAY 18

Regulating emotions

"Emotion-regulation leads to life-regulation."

Sam Owen

Emotions are the meaning we give to our body's sensations. This interpretation is shaped by the context we are currently in *and* our past. Meaning, two people feeling the same bodily sensation within the same context might experience different emotional states based on their individual past experiences.

Let's take the sensation of an increased heart rate as an example and see how it can be interpreted in various ways based on the context. For instance, in a situation of conflict, it could be interpreted as anger or fear; before giving a speech, as excitement or nervousness; when confronting someone who intimidates us, as courage or fear; when training for cardiovascular health, as accomplishment or exhaustion; when about to say goodbye to a loved one, as sadness or loneliness; and when reuniting with someone we love, as excitement or happiness. In all these examples, the physical sensation of an increased heart rate remains the same, but the emotional experience is completely different because of the context.

The power of context in shaping our emotions is pretty obvious. What is less obvious is the role our past experiences play in shaping our emotions. How is it that two people can be in the exact same context and have two different experiences? Let me use some of the examples above to show you how the same situation might elicit different emotions in different people. For example, a situation of conflict or confrontation can be terrifying for someone who grew up in an environment where conflict or confrontation usually ended up in violence, whereas for someone who experienced safety in most relationships, it could be a constructive way of expressing disagreement and reinforcing boundaries. A public speaking opportunity might bring excitement to a performer with vast and positive experience of being in the spotlight, while a person with limited or unpleasant experiences of speaking in public might experience nervousness or even terror. When training for cardiovascular health, an athlete or a person focused on physical fitness would feel a sense of accomplishment when experiencing an increased heart rate, while someone who hasn't exercised for a while, but has been told they have to by their doctor, might feel dread or exhaustion.

Understanding how our emotions are shaped by the meaning we give to our physical sensations, based on the context and our past experiences, is empowering. Why? Because we can use this understanding to guide the steps that can change our emotional experience in real time. For example, we can tend to our body by providing comfort and all the necessary elements for proper functioning, we can identify and accurately label the emotional experience, and we can also differentiate between past and current experiences. The more flexible we are in our interpretation of physical sensations and our ability to discern between nuances, the more likely we are to maintain emotional balance.

Experiential activity

For today's practice, I invite you to take out your journal and a pen and find a quiet space where you can be comfortable and free from distractions. In this exercise, you will go through a sequence of steps designed to help you experience the process of emotion regulation. There will be several prompts for reflection, and after each prompt, I invite you to close your eyes for a few moments, allowing yourself to reflect on your answers. Before you start, take a few deep breaths, letting go of any unnecessary tension in your body.

Now I invite you to think of something that is currently upsetting or bothering you. For the purpose of this practice, think of something mild, such as being left out of a conversation, a friend canceling on you last minute, a mistake you made, a recent argument, or missing a deadline. Once you have the situation clear in your mind, I invite you to identify any physical discomfort that might accompany this experience. For instance, heaviness or lightness in your arms and legs, a faster heartbeat, tightness in your chest, shallow breathing, increased warmth or coolness in your body, stiffness in your shoulders, a knot in your stomach, or tension in your head. If, at any point, the sensations in your body become overwhelming, use an anchoring strategy to ground yourself in the present moment, or completely disengage from the exercise.

Tend to your body

Once you've identified the areas of tension or discomfort, I invite you to place a hand, or both hands, on those areas (e.g., your heart, stomach, chest, shoulders, forehead) and apply gentle pressure. Feel the warmth of your hands and use this moment to offer yourself kindness and support. If it feels good, move your hand in small, circular motions on the tense areas, offering a sense of comfort. With each breath, bring ease into the areas of tension, and with each exhale, relax that part of the body. You may close your eyes and use your inner voice to whisper softly to yourself loving and supportive phrases, such as "I am safe in this moment," "It's okay to not have everything figured out," "I will find my way," "I deserve kindness and understanding, just like anyone else," or "I am here for you."

Identify and label your emotion

Now I invite you to label the emotion you are experiencing by using specific language. For example, instead of just saying "bad" or "upset," try to identify the nuance of your emotion, such as disappointment, worry, regret, resentment, guilt, sadness, frustration, or jealousy.

Take your journal out and write the answer to this question: *What is the most accurate label for how I'm feeling right now?* Sometimes, emotions are complex and layered. If more than one emotion is present, note each one, but try to start with the most dominant. Take a few moments to simply be with this emotion—there is no need to rush through this process. With each breath, imagine you are breathing in compassion for yourself and breathing out tension or discomfort. Continue to offer your body support until you notice a shift in your physical experience. The goal here is not to eliminate the emotion but to create space for it with self-compassion.

Differentiate the present from the past

Now I invite you to reflect on whether this emotion is directly related to your present circumstances or whether it feels amplified by memories of similar painful experiences. Take a moment to recognize that although this current emotional experience feels similar to the ones in the past, they are not identical. Remind yourself that this present moment, although familiar, is different from the past. You are not in the same situation you may have experienced before. You have grown, and you are now better equipped with knowledge and tools than ever before to manage challenges differently.

Now write in your journal the answer to this question: *Is my emotional response to this situation based only on current events, or am I responding to what is going on right now **plus** all similar painful situations from my past?* As you differentiate between the past and the present, see if you notice any shift in emotions or any changes in how the emotion feels in your body.

Before closing this practice, take a few more deep breaths, releasing any unnecessary tension in your body. When you are ready, give yourself permission to move forward with your day, carrying with you the awareness that your emotions are valid and you have the ability to navigate them with compassion and presence. Also, remember that emotions are ever-changing, like clouds drifting in the sky.

Feel free to return to this exercise whenever you're experiencing strong emotions, and know that, with practice, you will build a deeper capacity for emotion regulation.

DAY 19

I am choosing what feels good

*"Living mindfully, slowing down and enjoying each step
and each breath, is enough."*

Thich Nhat Hanh

We can expand our positive experiences by choosing what feels good to us. Each day, we can choose, with intention, what brings us joy, laughter, comfort, connection, peace, freedom, hope, or inspiration—all pleasant experiences that add to the quality of our life. Choosing what feels good won't make life's difficulties disappear, but it can bring ease amid those challenges. It can also enhance life when it already feels good.

What feels good will differ each day based on your needs. For example, a nap might feel good on a day when you are tired, a delicious meal on a day when you feel hungry, a run when you need to connect with your body or clear your mind, a comedy show when you could use a good laugh, hanging out with a friend when you long for connection, reading a novel when you crave an adventure, cleaning the house when you need order, good music when you feel playful and want to dance, or making a decision when you need to change something in your life. The list can go on and on depending on your unique needs and desires.

When we choose what feels good, whether it is meeting an immediate need, helping others, or making a decision about life, we're more likely to maintain a pleasant state because we are doing things that truly matter to us. It is also a form of self-trust because we acknowledge that we know ourselves best; we know our needs, dreams, and desires better than anyone else. Over time, choosing what feels good strengthens our ability to make empowered decisions that maintain a state of balance and wellbeing.

So, today, I invite you to give yourself overt permission to choose what feels good to you. For some, choosing what feels good might be difficult because it might feel like selfishness or indulgence. If that is the case for you, acknowledge that belief and examine it with gentleness and curiosity; wonder where you might have received that message and how that belief has formed for you. See if you can put it aside today and still choose what feels good. Over time, your brain will take all these new positive experiences and create new predictions that will increase the quality of your daily life.

Experiential activity

For today's practice, I invite you to take a few moments and think about what would feel good to you today—for example, something that would meet an immediate need (e.g., eating a delicious nutritious meal, resting, seeking comfort, cleaning) or bring pleasure (e.g., listening to music, walking in nature, reading a book, baking) or meaning (e.g., helping others, engaging in a hobby, creating something). Whatever feels good, choose that today.

If you find yourself struggling to identify what feels good, refer to the list of things you identified as feeling good to you on day seven of this journey. You can always use that list as a guide to remind you of all the things that make you feel good. Each day, you can choose at least one thing from that list to add pleasant experiences into your daily life.

DAY 20

One-minute noticing

*"Clarity and decisiveness come from the willingness to slow down,
to listen to and look at what's happening."*

Pema Chödrön

I often hear people say they don't have time to meditate or reflect on their experiences. We are indeed living in busy and demanding times, making us feel as if we have no space to breathe, let alone meditate. With that in mind, I want to introduce you to the **one-minute noticing** practice, which can transform your day-to-day experience for the better. This practice creates space in our demanding lives to consistently check in with ourselves and, as a result, become aware of our body, mind, and emotional states. Why is this awareness important? Because the only things we can change are the ones we are aware of, and the only pains we can tend to are the ones we create space for, to feel.

Experiential activity

For today's practice, I invite you to turn your attention inward with genuine curiosity. The aim is to bring your physical, mental, and emotional states into your awareness, without any intention to change anything. This practice requires only five minutes of your day, divided into one-minute intervals.

Wherever you are and whatever you are doing, I invite you to pause for one minute and check in with yourself with genuine care, as you would with a dear friend, and with no intent to change a thing. Start by noticing how your body feels in this very moment, whether it feels rested or tired, hungry or full. Notice if there is tension or pain in any areas of your body, or if perhaps your body feels relaxed. If you would like, instead of focusing on your body, you can take this minute to observe your thoughts. Are they happy or hopeful thoughts? Fearful or critical thoughts? Are they repeating the same story over and over again? Whatever the case, just notice. You can also choose to observe your feelings during this minute of practice.

Are you feeling content, grateful, playful, valued, excited, curious, loving, inspired? Or maybe you feel scared, insecure, ashamed, betrayed, excluded, overwhelmed, guilty, or jealous. You might feel a combination of similar emotions or maybe conflicting ones. Whatever the case, just observe them for one full minute.

This is a practice you can implement first thing in the morning. You can take one minute to turn your attention inward while still lying in bed or sitting on the side of your bed just before stepping into the day. Then, go on with your day and repeat the one minute of noticing at noon or right before your lunch. Later, when you get home from work, before or after you get in the house, pause for another minute to observe your experience. Repeat the one minute of noticing around dinner time, and then one more time before you go to sleep.

You can create your own structure for the one minute of noticing, one that fits around your daily activities. There might be times in your day other than those mentioned above that work better for you. You can also set up an alarm five times a day to remind you of your practice. Find a rhythm that works for you, and as you are progressing in your practice, you will find it becomes easier and easier to maintain that rhythm.

The purpose of this experience is to observe with curiosity and without any judgment what is going on for you in that particular moment. As the day progresses, you might observe changes in your body, thoughts, and emotions. Over time, this practice will increase your awareness of daily experiences, both pleasant and unpleasant ones. When the experiences are pleasant, savor them, and when they are unpleasant, offer yourself kind words of support.

DAY 21

Slowing down to savor life

"Achieving isn't living. Living is living."

Bill Burr

We live in a world where constant busyness is seen as a sign of success or productivity. We are racing against time, trying to juggle work, family, social life, and endless to-do lists, always in a state of motion, checking off boxes, and continuously *doing* something. It's almost like the goal is not just to live anymore, but rather to optimize every single moment of the day.

We have this underlying belief that if we are not constantly working or improving, we are somehow falling behind, as if we are not doing enough or moving fast enough. The rush of life can make us go through the motions, missing out on the richness of simple moments. This rush steals from us the very things that bring us joy, such as the moments of connection, quiet reflection, or relaxation. Instead of enjoying a slow morning, a peaceful evening, or an uneventful weekend, we have a need to fill the time with activities, as if silence and stillness are things to avoid.

Slowing down, even just a little, can make a big difference in how we experience life. When we slow down, we create space to focus on what's truly important, process our experiences, reflect, and make better decisions. Slowing down helps us savor life instead of just moving through it. It creates room to enjoy simple things, like a slow walk, a good meal, sipping coffee, or a moment of peace. When we slow down, we become more attuned to our senses and the world around us. We notice the warmth of the sun on our face, the smell of fresh rain, the taste of a home-cooked meal, the smile of a stranger, or the beauty of a flower.

Slowing down is not just about taking breaks; it is about giving ourselves permission to not always be busy. Our body needs time to rest, and our brain needs time to process and recharge. We need space for stillness and to daydream. We need time to play. Some of the best ideas come when we step away from the noise and let our minds wander. Taking walks, journaling, or even just having some quiet time can lead to sudden bursts of inspiration. Slowing down means we can dive deeper, whether that is into your work, play, or relationships.

Slowing down also gives us more time to really engage with those around us. Have you ever had a conversation where you felt like the other person was *really* listening? Isn't it such a meaningful experience to be truly present with the person in front of you? Listening, eye contact, and empathy are all enhanced when we slow down and become present. It gives us the space to nurture the connections that matter most and show up in a way that's meaningful.

Today's focus is on slowing down and intentionally choosing what matters most. Today is about *doing* less and *being* more. You will be stepping back to make sure that you are moving at a pace that actually allows you to savor life rather than just moving through it. Today, you will move with no rush and no pressure, just mindful actions that bring peace, comfort, and joy. Today you will catch your breath and reconnect with yourself.

Experiential activity

To start today's practice, I invite you to take a few deep breaths, inhaling deeply and exhaling slowly a few times, starting to prepare for a slower pace. You can close your eyes and allow your body to relax. After taking a few deep breaths and releasing any unnecessary tension in your body, I invite you to set your intention for the day to be fully present and savor the little moments. You can whisper to yourself something simple like "Today, I choose to be present" or "Today, I will savor the little moments."

As you are going through your day, moving from one task to another, remind yourself that you have the power to choose how you move through it. Take breaks throughout the day, closing your eyes and taking deep breaths, sitting quietly and noticing how your body feels, relaxing your body and letting go of all the tension you might have accumulated up to that point. As you are moving through the day, avoid the temptation to rush, letting your movement set a calm tone for your day. However slowly you find yourself going, see if you can slow down even more. Notice how your body feels and make space for some gentle stretching to support your body throughout the day.

Put all screens away and your phone on silent. Leave your phone in another room, unless you absolutely need it for emergencies. Step away from technology and let all the digital noise fade away. Instead, choose something more grounding, such as sitting outside, taking a slow walk, reading a book, writing in a journal, or simply resting and letting your mind wander.

During mealtimes, take your time eating, focusing entirely on your meal, noticing the textures, the flavors, and the feeling of each bite. Enjoy the experience of nourishing your body without rushing.

Go outside, even if it's just for a few minutes. Take a walk or simply sit and observe nature around you, allowing yourself to be fully immersed in the natural world. Feel the wind on your face, listen to the birds, notice the colors around you. Step outside as the sun sets and witness nature transitioning for nighttime. And just like nature, let yourself transition from the pace of the day to a restful evening without rushing. Dim the lights, take a warm bath, or simply listen to soft music, avoiding screens or anything stimulating.

As the evening sets in, take your journal out and find a quiet space to reflect on your day. Write in your journal the answer to the following questions:

- Have you noticed moments of slowness and ease?

- What were the moments when you were truly present?

- What were the moments you enjoyed the most?

- What were the moments you are grateful for?

Slow living is a practice, and today is just the beginning. Let this day serve as a reminder that life doesn't have to be rushed, and slowing down doesn't mean doing less; it means being intentional with the moments we have. Each mindful moment gradually enhances the quality of your daily experiences, and eventually your quality of life.

A Final Word

Sustaining and Deepening Your Practice

"Wherever you go, there you are."

Jon Kabat-Zinn

Congratulations! You've done it! You've taken your first steps on the lifelong journey of self-regulation. You've learned how we form our view of the world and why we experience the world as we do. You've practiced the ART of self-regulation and experienced the power of the strategies you can use when things become challenging. You now have tools you could draw upon during turbulent times, or when you simply want to reconnect to the present moment and savor the good things in your life. You understand your attachment style, and you know how to identify and reflect on your thoughts and emotions with curiosity and care, listening closely to your inner dialogue. You've practiced ways to create new and positive experiences that will fuel other positive experiences, eventually leading to a pleasant life.

The adventure isn't over

All the knowledge and skills you have accumulated through this book will serve as a foundation for all the future knowledge and skills you will continue to build up over your lifetime. There is no end point to the practice of self-regulation—it truly is a lifelong journey. Rest assured, life will give you plenty of opportunities to practice the ART of self-regulation, so completing the 21-day practical guide is not the finish line, but a building block within a continuous process of evolution.

What comes next in this continuous process of development? you might wonder. The answer is: it depends. It is all based on your own needs and wants. There is no right or wrong way to move into your next meaningful actions. Your way will always be the best way. So, at this point, you might decide to take some time and continue practicing the ART of self-regulation, creating space for a consistent practice of sitting meditation, movement, and journaling, or slowing down and savoring the good things that are already part of your life. If you would like to dive deeper into the practice of self-compassion, the eight-week 'Mindful Self-Compassion' program, developed by Kristin Neff and Chris Germer, would be a great next step to take.

On the other hand, you might consider deepening your understanding of your *self* by acknowledging and healing those parts that have been hurt or neglected over time. Individual psychotherapy with a licensed mental health professional could provide the space and support for such a healing journey.

You can also gain more knowledge from authors and teachers that have researched, practiced, and guided others toward a more meaningful life. Below is a list of books and powerful thinkers, teachers, and authors that can guide your steps forward.

Guiding books

- *Attached* – Amir Levine and Rachel Heller
- *How Emotions Are Made* – Lisa Feldman Barrett
- *In Praise of Slowness* – Carl Honoré
- *Mindsight* – Dan Siegel
- *Protocols* – Andrew D. Huberman

- *Radical Acceptance* – Tara Brach
- *Self-Compassion* – Kristin Neff
- *Seven and a Half Lessons About the Brain* – Lisa Feldman Barrett
- *Shame and Guilt* – June Price Tangney and Ronda L. Dearing
- *Start Where You Are* – Pema Chödrön
- *A Compelling Idea* – L. Alan Sroufe
- *The Mindful Path to Self-Compassion* – Christopher Germer
- *The Power of Now* – Eckhart Tolle
- *The Power of Vulnerability* – Brené Brown
- *The Self-Compassion Workbook* – Kristin Neff and Christopher Germer

Mentors of the mind and heart

- Adriene Mishler – yogawithadriene.com
- Andrew Huberman – hubermanlab.com
- Brené Brown – brenebrown.com
- Christopher Germer – chrisgermer.com
- Dalai Lama – dalailama.com
- Dan Siegel – drdansiegel.com
- Gabor Maté – drgabormate.com
- Jon Kabat-Zinn – jonkabat-zinn.com
- Kristin Neff – self-compassion.org
- Lisa Feldman Barrett – lisafeldmanbarrett.com
- Peter A. Levine – somaticexperiencing.com
- Tara Brach – tarabrach.com

About the Author

"Every artist was first an amateur."

Ralph Waldo Emerson

Nicoleta Dragan has dedicated her professional life to guiding others toward emotional wellbeing. She holds a master's degree in clinical psychology and a doctorate in educational leadership. Nicoleta approaches emotional wellbeing from a holistic perspective, emphasizing the vital role education plays in mental health.

Nicoleta is a licensed marriage and family therapist and a credentialed school psychologist. For more than a decade, she has worked as a psychotherapist, clinical supervisor, and mental health educator across a variety of settings. Currently, she holds the position of mental health program specialist for a large school district in Southern California. In addition to her work in schools, she teaches psychology at a local community college, leads mental health-related workshops, and speaks on topics such as self-regulation and self-compassion.

Nicoleta's work is influenced by the science of attachment, shame, self-compassion, and neuroscience. She approaches these topics with an understanding rooted not only in science but also in lived experiences—both her own and that of the many individuals she has supported. Her insights are shaped by years of therapeutic work, where she has witnessed the positive impact of these concepts in everyday life. She has also conducted and published a research study examining the links between early experiences, shame, capacity for emotion regulation, and levels of self-compassion, offering valuable insights into how our earliest experiences shape the way we relate to ourselves.

Whether through writing, teaching, or psychotherapy, Nicoleta's mission is to empower individuals and communities to take charge of their emotional wellbeing. She creates spaces where wellbeing is openly discussed, understood, and nurtured. She is committed to spreading the message of self-regulation, self-compassion, and other pillars of wellbeing in a manner accessible and practical for all. *The ART of Self-Regulation* is a reflection of this mission and a tangible expression of her passion.

Website: nicoletadragan.com

Instagram: @drnicoletadragan

YouTube: @nicoleta.dragan

Bibliography

> "If I have seen further, it is by standing on the shoulders of giants."
>
> *Isaac Newton*

Arch, J. J., Brown, K. W., Dean, D. J., Landy, L. N., Brown, K. D., & Laudenslager, M. L. (2014). Self-compassion training modulates alpha-amylase, heart rate variability, and subjective responses to social evaluative threat in women. *Psychoneuroendocrinology*, 42, 49–58.

Arslan, C. (2016). Interpersonal problem solving, self-compassion and personality traits in university students. *Educational Research and Reviews*, 11(7), 474–81.

Atzil, S., & Barrett, L. F. (2017). Social regulation of allostasis: Commentary on "Mentalizing homeostasis: The social origins of interoceptive inference" by Fotopoulou and Tsakiris. *Neuropsychoanalysis*, 19(1), 29–33.

Balban, M. Y., Neri, E., Kogon, M. M., Weed, L., Nouriani, B., Jo, B., Holl, G., Zeitzer, J. M., Spiegel, D., & Huberman, A. D. (2023). Brief structured respiration practices enhance mood and reduce physiological arousal. *Cell Reports Medicine*, 4(1).

Barrett, L. F. (2017). *How emotions are made: The secret life of the brain*. Houghton Mifflin Harcourt.

Barrett, L. F. (2020). *Seven and a Half Lessons About the Brain*. Houghton Mifflin Harcourt.

Barrett, L. F., & Simmons, W. K. (2015). Interoceptive predictions in the brain. *Nature Reviews Neuroscience*, 16(7), 419–29.

Barrett, L. F., Mesquita, B., Ochsner, K. N., & Gross, J. J. (2007). The experience of emotion. *Annual Review of Psychology*, 58(1), 373–403.

Bell, M. A. (2020). Mother-child behavioral and physiological synchrony. *Advances in Child Development and Behavior*, 58, 163–88.

Bishop, S. R., Lau, M., Shapiro, S., Carlson, L., Anderson, N. D., Carmody, J., Segal, Z. V., Abbey, S., Speca, M., Velting, D., & Devins, G. (2004). Mindfulness: A proposed operational definition. *Clinical Psychology: Science and Practice*, 11(3), 230-241.

Breines, J. G., McInnis, C. M., Kuras, Y. I., Thoma, M. V., Gianferante, D., Hanlin, L., Chen, X., & Rohleder, N. (2015). Self-compassionate young adults show lower salivary alpha-amylase responses to repeated psychosocial stress. *Self and Identity*, 14(4), 1–13.

Bryant, F. B. (2021). Current progress and future directions for theory and research on savoring. *Frontiers in psychology*, 12, 771698.

Bryant, F. B., & Veroff, J. (2017). Savoring: A new model of positive experience. *Psychology Press*.

Cassidy, J., & Shaver, P. R. (Eds.). (2016). *Handbook of Attachment: Theory, Research, and Clinical Applications* (3rd ed.). The Guilford Press.

Creswell, J. D., Way, B. M., Eisenberger, N. I., & Lieberman, M. D. (2007). Neural correlates of dispositional mindfulness during affect labeling. *Biopsychosocial Science and Medicine*, 69(6), 560-565.

Dragan, N., Kamptner, L., & Riggs, M. (2021). The impact of the early caregiving environment on self-compassion: The mediating effects of emotion regulation and shame. *Mindfulness*, 12(7), 1708–18.

Ehret, A. M., Joormann, J, & Berking, M. (2015). Examining risk and resilience factors for depression: The role of self-criticism and self-compassion. *Cognition and Emotions*, 29(8). 1496–1504.

Ferreira, C., Pinto-Gouveia, J., & Duarte, C. (2013). Self-compassion in the face of shame and body image dissatisfaction: Implications for eating disorders. *Eating Behaviors*, 14, 207–10.

Fredrickson, B. L. (2004). The broaden–and–build theory of positive emotions. *Philosophical transactions of the royal society of London. Series B: Biological Sciences*, 359(1449), 1367-1377.

Friis, A. M., Johnson, M. H., Cutfield, R. G., & Consedine, N. S. (2015). Does kindness matter? Self-compassion buffers the negative impact of diabetes-distress on HbA1c. *Diabetic Medicine*, 32(12),1634–40.

Friis, A. M., Johnson, M. H., Cutfield, R. G., & Consedine, N. S. (2016). Kindness matters: A randomized controlled trial of a mindful self-compassion intervention improves depression, distress, and HbA1c among patients with diabetes. *Diabetes Care*, 39(11), 1963–71.

Galla, B. M. (2016). Within-person changes in mindfulness and self-compassion predict enhanced emotional well-being in healthy, but stressed adolescents. *Journal of Adolescence*, 49, 204–17.

Gerber, Z., Tolmacz, R., & Doron, Y. (2015). Self-compassion and forms of concern for others. *Personality and Individual Differences*, 86, 394–400.

Germer, C. (2009). *The mindful path to self-compassion: Freeing yourself from destructive thoughts and emotions*. Guilford Press.

Gilbert, P. (2009). Introducing compassion-focused therapy. *Advances in psychiatric treatment*, 15(3), 199-208.

Grille, R. (2014). *Parenting for a Peaceful World*. New Society Publishers.

Gunnell, K. E., Mosewich, A. D., McEwen, C. E., Eklund, R. C., & Crocker, P. R. (2017). Don't be so hard on yourself! Changes in self-compassion during the first year of university are associated with changes in well-being. *Personality and Individual Differences*, 107, 43–8.

Hanson, R. (2013). *Hardwiring Happiness: The Practical Science of Reshaping Your Brain-and Your Life*. Random House.

Homan, K. J. (2016). Self-compassion and psychological well-being in older adults. *Journal of Adult Development*, 23(2), 111–19.

Hope, N., Koestner, R., & Milyavskaya, M. (2014). The role of self-compassion in goal pursuit and well-being among university freshmen. *Self and Identity*, 12(5), 579–93.

Jose, P. E., Lim, B. T., & Bryant, F. B. (2012). Does savoring increase happiness? A daily diary study. *The Journal of Positive Psychology*, 7(3), 176-187.

Krejtz, I., Nezlek, J. B., Michnicka, A., Holas, P., & Rusanowska, M. (2016). Counting one's blessings can reduce the impact of daily stress. *Journal of Happiness Studies*, 17(1), 25-39.

Levine, A., & Heller, R. (2010). *Attached: The New Science of Adult Attachment and How It Can Help You Find--and Keep--Love*. Penguin.

MacBeth, A., & Gumley, A. (2012). Exploring compassion: A meta-analysis of the association between self-compassion and psychopathology. *Clinical Psychology Review*, 32(6), 545–52.

Marshall, E. J., & Brockman, R. N. (2016). The relationships between psychological flexibility, self-compassion, and emotional well-being. *Journal of Cognitive Psychotherapy*, 30(1), 60–72.

Mikulincer, M., & Shaver, P. R. (2004). Security-based self-representations in adulthood. *Adult Attachment: Theory, Research, and Clinical Implications*, 159–95.

Mikulincer, M., & Shaver, P. R. (2007). *Attachment in Adulthood: Structure, Dynamics, and Change*. The Guilford Press.

Miller, K. J., & Clark, A. (2018). Happily entangled: Prediction error and associative learning theory. *Cognitive, Affective, & Behavioral Neuroscience*, 18(3), 465–78.

Neff, K. (2003). Self-compassion: An alternative conceptualization of a healthy attitude toward oneself. *Self and Identity*, 2(2), 85–101.

Neff, K. (2011). *Self-compassion: The proven power of being kind to yourself.* Hachette UK.

Neff, K. D. (2023). Self-compassion: Theory, method, research, and intervention. *Annual Review of Psychology*, 74(1), 193–218.

Neff, K. D., & Beretvas, S. N. (2013). The role of self-compassion in romantic relationships. *Self and Identity*, 12(1), 78–98.

Neff, K. D., & McGehee, P. (2010). Self-compassion and psychological resilience among adolescents and young adults. *Self and Identity*, 9, 225–40.

Neff, K. D., & Vonk, R. (2009). Self-compassion versus global self-esteem: Two different ways of relating to oneself. *Journal of Personality*, 77(1), 23–50.

Powell, S. K. (2022). The science of gratitude. *Professional Case Management*, 27(6), 261-262.

Remondi, C., Casu, G., Pozzi, C., Greco, F., Gremigni, P., & Brugnera, A. (2023). A serial mediation model of insecure attachment and psychological distress: The role of dispositional shame and shame-coping styles. *International Journal of Environmental Research and Public Health*, 20(4), 3193.

Rozin, P., & Royzman, E. B. (2001). Negativity bias, negativity dominance, and contagion. *Personality and social psychology review*, 5(4), 296-320.

Rueda, M. R., Moyano, S., & Rico-Picó, J. (2023). Attention: The grounds of self-regulated cognition. *Wiley Interdisciplinary Reviews: Cognitive Science*, 14(1), e1582.

Sedighimornani, N., Rimes, K., & Verplanken, B. (2021). Factors contributing to the experience of shame and shame management: Adverse childhood experiences, peer acceptance, and attachment styles. *The Journal of Social Psychology*, 161(2), 129–45.

Siegel, D. J. (2012). *The Developing Mind: How Relationships and the Brain Interact to Shape Who We Are* (2nd ed.). The Guilford Press.

Siegel, D. J. (2010). *Mindsight: The new science of personal transformation.* Bantam.

Shonkoff, J. P., Phillips, D. A., & National Research Council. (2000). Acquiring self-regulation. In *From Neurons to Neighborhoods: The Science of Early Childhood Development*. National Academies Press (US).

Sroufe, L. A. (2021). *A Compelling Idea: How We Become the Persons We Are.* Safer Society Press.

Sroufe, L. A., Egeland, B., Carlson, E. A., & Collins, W. A. (2005). *The Development of the Person: The Minnesota Study of Risk and Adaptation from Birth to Adulthood.* The Guilford Press.

Svendsen, J. L., Osnes, B., Binder, P. E., Dundas, I., Visted, E., Nordby, H., Schanche, E. & Sørensen, L. (2016). Trait self-compassion reflects emotional flexibility through an association with high vagally mediated heart rate variability. *Mindfulness,* 7(5), 1103–13.

Tangney, J. P., & Dearing, R. L. (2003). *Shame and Guilt.* Guilford Press.

Timmons, L. N. (2018). *Facial Affect and Physiological Synchrony during Parent-infant Interactions and Influences on Later Developmental Outcomes.* Texas Christian University.

Ullrich, P. M., & Lutgendorf, S. K. (2002). Journaling about stressful events: Effects of cognitive processing and emotional expression. *Annals of behavioral medicine,* 24(3), 244-250.

Wadlinger, H. A., & Isaacowitz, D. M. (2011). Fixing our focus: Training attention to regulate emotion. *Personality and social psychology review,* 15(1), 75-102.

Wood, A. M., Froh, J. J., & Geraghty, A. W. (2010). Gratitude and well-being: A review and theoretical integration. *Clinical psychology review,* 30(7), 890-905.

Yang, Y., Zhang, M., & Kou, Y. (2016). Self-compassion and life satisfaction: The mediating role of hope. *Personality and Individual Differences,* 98, 91–5.

Yarnell, L. M., & Neff, K. D. (2013). Self-compassion, interpersonal conflict resolutions, and well-being. *Self and Identity,* 12(2), 146–59.

Zeller, M., Yuval, K., Nitzan-Assayag, Y., & Bernstein, A. (2014). Self-compassion in recovery following potentially traumatic stress: Longitudinal study of at-risk youth. *Journal of Abnormal Child Psychology,* 1–9.

Zessin, U., Dickhäuser, O., & Garbade, S. (2015). The relationship between self-compassion and well-being: A meta-analysis. *Applied Psychology: Health and Well-Being,* 7(3), 340–64.

Zimmerman, B. J. (2000). Attaining self-regulation: A social cognitive perspective'. In M. Boekaerts, P. R. Pintrich, & M. Zeidner (Eds.) *Handbook of Self-Regulation* (pp. 13–39). Academic Press.